To Grandma

Christmas
1999

From Michelle & Sharon

A Gift
of Miracles

Other books by Jamie C. Miller, Laura Lewis,
and Jennifer Basye Sander

Christmas Miracles
The Magic of Christmas Miracles
Mothers' Miracles

A Gift
of Miracles

MAGICAL TRUE
STORIES TO TOUCH YOUR
FAMILY'S HEART

Jamie C. Miller, Laura Lewis, and
Jennifer Basye Sander

WILLIAM MORROW AND COMPANY, INC.

NEW YORK

It is the policy of William Morrow and Company, Inc., and its imprints and affiliates, recognizing the importance of preserving what has been written, to print the books we publish on acid-free paper, and we exert our best efforts to that end.

Library of Congress Cataloging-in-Publication Data has been applied for.

ISBN 0-688-17369-1

Printed in the United States of America

First Edition

1 2 3 4 5 6 7 8 9 10

BOOK DESIGN BY JO ANNE METSCH

www.williammorrow.com

The only gift is a portion of thyself.

—Ralph Waldo Emerson

Contents

INTRODUCTION · 1

A SPECIAL REQUEST · *Frank Baranowski* · 5

PAUL AND THE PUPPIES · *Lucy Whitsett McGuire* · 11

THE SEARCH FOR MARY · *Helen Kinzeler* · 16

RUNNING ON INSTINCT · *Reda Wallace* · 22

THE BIRTH OF A FATHER · *Debbie McLellan* · 27

SHOWERS OF BLESSING · *Victoria Hansen* · 32

THE FAMILY ACROSS THE WAY · *Rusty Fischer* · 41

COMFORT MY CHILDREN · *Mette Hansen Schaer* · 47

FINDING MY BESHERT · *Azriela Jaffe* · 51

THE CHRISTMAS COAT · *George E. Raley, Jr.* · 55

A LIFE TO SAVE · *John Pitcavage* · 60

A PERFECT POT OF TEA · *Roberta L. Messner* · 66

Contents

PAPA! · *Gil Sanchez* · 74

THE GIFT OF SILENCE · *Bobby Gawthrop* · 82

THE MIRACLE ON SHERBROOKE STREET
Stephen Laudi · 87

LINKS TO LOVE · *Jane Blevins* · 90

RADIO DAYS · *Cookie Curci-Wright* · 97

THE USHER · *John Richard* · 103

BLESSINGS FROM SAINT PETER
Edward Andrusko · 109

THE BRACELET PROMISE · *Carmen Leal-Pock* · 115

VISIONS OF MICHAEL · *Michael Stein* · 121

THE QUIET MAN · *Margaret H. Scanlon* · 127

THE FLIGHT OF OUR LIVES · *Julia Kelly* · 131

MILES DAVIS AND THE CARDBOARD MAN
Edward Rosmond · 136

SANTA WAS A JEWISH SHOPKEEPER
Marie Foley Nielsen · 141

HIGH SCHOOL REUNION · *Charles P. Perry* · 145

JOHANNA AND EMILY · *Michael DeSimone* · 151

REBECCA'S TOUCH · *Cynthia Stewart-Copier* · 156

BEYOND THE CALL OF DUTY · *Robert Mohr* · 162

THE SEARCH FOR ISRAEL · *Carol Ritenour* · 166

GOD'S PERFECT GIFT · *Mary Leisy* · 170

ACKNOWLEDGMENTS · 176

A Gift of Miracles

INTRODUCTION

miracle n. 1. *An event that seems impossible to explain by natural laws and so is regarded as supernatural in origin or as an act of God.* 2. *One that excites admiration or awe.*
—WEBSTER'S II RIVERSIDE DICTIONARY

N ANY GIVEN day in stores and malls across the country, millions of people shop for gifts. A mother looks for just the right gift for her daughter's sixteenth birthday. A husband searches for a sentimental gift to express love on his first wedding anniversary. Children shop for Mother's and Father's Day presents and lovers seek the perfect Valentine's Day gift. We celebrate marriages, the birth of babies, graduations, and religious holidays by giving the gifts we so carefully select for family and friends.

And then there is Christmas—the holiday in which more gifts are lovingly exchanged throughout the world than at any other time of year. The gifts we give at Christmas especially remind us of the wonder of giving and receiving, as we ponder the original gifts given by the three wise men to the Christ child. From the humble surroundings of a Bethlehem stable, we accept a tiny baby's birth as God's greatest gift of all—a true miracle to those who believe.

But unlike the gifts that are exchanged on specific holidays and special occasions, the gift of miracles can be given at any time, for no reason at all. In this, our latest collection of inspiring true stories, you will read touching accounts of the miraculous gifts given by those who allow their lives to be intricately woven with those around them. Like the best things in life, these gifts are unexpected, and are received with humility and joy.

Some miracles can only be explained by looking to God; they come about through some kind of divine intervention we don't fully comprehend. But what about miracles that occur when we simply respond to what our souls invite us to do—those that spring from an encouraging word to the lonely, a thoughtful card, a gentle touch, a smile, a few minutes of patient listening? Can common people really create miracles in the lives of others? After hundreds of hours of listening to tales of the wondrous—to miracles that, at their very core, have sprung from a human hand—we believe people can.

How else to explain the man who overcomes his own depression by donating a very special winter coat to a homeless man? How else to explain the determined mother whose gift of devotion helps her crippled son first learn to walk, then run, all the way to a record-breaking college football career? Or what about the dying man who, after receiving two anonymous letters through the mail, is able to give his wife one last precious gift?

In story after story, we learn that often these gifts have the greatest meaning when we need them—in dark times, when we feel we've lost touch with ourselves or others. A great pioneer leader once compared life to a huge wagon wheel. Like the spokes on the wheel, all of us at times will find ourselves pointed downward, at the bottom, needing someone to pull us up. But as life evolves, like the revolving wheel, there will be times when we're at the top of the wheel, pointing heavenward, and we can reach down and help lift others up. These are the times when we can encourage and inspire and create real miracles for those who have done the same for us, or may, at some future time in our own low moments.

Consider the simple miracle of the daffodils. A woman living in the Midwest tells about a time in her life when various commitments kept her extremely busy and on a demanding schedule, with much time spent away from her home and family. Although she loved being around the house to cook and tend her garden, it was necessary to leave town for several weeks during the period when she normally would have planted tulip bulbs and daffodils in her front yard. She felt sad as she looked at the dark earth and realized that no bulbs would burst forth to announce spring that year. On a somewhat lonely birthday in March, however, she walked out into her yard and saw three daffodils. She wondered how that had happened. When had they bloomed and who had planted them? The next day there were more daffodils. Before long, she discovered tulips. They sprang up every day in different places, and every morning she ran out to see what was coming up out of the ground, which to her knowledge was void of bulbs or seeds.

Those seeds of love had been planted in the fall by a

friend. Different plants continued coming up to delight and surprise her for about two weeks, and then an anonymous card arrived: "Happy Birthday! I thought the flowers would be an announcement of spring and I wanted to warm your heart this spring." It was a simple gift from a caring friend, but a miracle of hope and joy to the receiver, and one she would never forget.

On those days—and we all have them—when we may feel useless or worthless, unfulfilled, or maybe bored or lonely, reaching out to plant seeds of love in the lives of others will bring meaning to our own. As we push beyond the borders of our comfort zones to give the most enduring gift—the gift of self—we will be richly rewarded.

This collection of heartwarming stories is a gift to be unwrapped gently and carefully. As you go from one story to the next, like unfolding the layers of tissue paper inside a gift box, we hope you will savor the message of each simple or extraordinary miracle that has somehow changed a person's life. There are many gifts to be treasured in these accounts— the gift of faith, the gifts of love and devotion, the gift of a belief in the kindness of others. But perhaps it is the hope that such miraculous events kindle, the belief that they can really come out of the blue at any moment of our lives—that is the greatest gift of all.

Please do share your miracle stories with us. Contact: Miracles, P.O. Box 2463, Granite Bay, CA 95746.

—JAMIE,
LAURA,
AND JENNIFER

A Special Request

E WERE BUSY. With Christmas just a handful of days away, every talk-show host at the station was searching for the best in radio programming. After all, Christmas is a magic time of the year. To help create a meaningful and memorable radio show for all your listeners, you want the pageantry, the glory, and the mystique of the season. So you dig, hoping to find some little-known fact or a new story to build on. But after nine years on the air in Phoenix, Arizona, with my show *Mysteries Around Us*, a program dealing with unexplained phenomena, I was scraping the bottom of the holiday story barrel.

Coming from the Midwest as I do, it is easy to remember the sights and sounds of my childhood holidays—snow-draped Christmas trees, caroling parties where the cold night air was filled with the sweet sound of German, Polish, and Italian carols. And the food. A good cook on any day, Mom outdid herself at holiday time. I have wonderful memories of holidays past, memories I treasure still.

Perhaps I could recreate that same experience for my listeners, I thought as I rummaged around for inspiration. I couldn't give anyone in Phoenix a snow-draped Christmas tree or cold night air, but the town does have a pretty diverse ethnic mix; folks have moved here from all corners of the world. I could put together a program of stories and music from many countries in the hope that it might rekindle memories of another time, another place, for some of the listeners out there. Little did I know how effective my plan would prove to be.

One of the songs I planned to use on the air was a traditional Polish carol: "Hush-a-Bye Wee Jesus." In Polish it's called "Lulajze Jezuniu." Would I even be able to find a recording of that? I wondered as I drew up my dream list of songs I'd like to play. But luck was with me, and I found a CD recording by a Canadian group known as the Billy Andrusco Trio. Two sisters, Sherry and Sheila Aldridge, do the vocals. And the CD had not one, but two recordings of the song, one with the words in English, one in Polish. My playlist was complete, and I settled in to do the show.

Moments after I played "Hush-a-Bye" on the air that night a call came in to our station's technical director. Would we please play the Polish version of the song again? And not just once, but over and over again?

I will admit that my first impulse was not in the spirit of giving—I wanted to shrug off the request. I'd put a lot of thought and effort into crafting this international musical tour. We had finished playing the music of Poland and were now well into the Christmas music of Germany. And not only that, but to play just the Polish version was impossible. You had to listen to the entire English version first.

But my moment of selfishness passed quickly, and I heard a quiet voice in my heart. Do it! the voice urged. Go ahead and grant someone a Christmas wish. Do it now! And so I did. I asked the director to fade out the German carols and slowly bring up "Hush-a-Bye." Not knowing the reason behind the odd request we'd received, I simply explained on the air that the song meant a lot to me. Which is actually true—my mother used to sing it to me when I was a small child.

My technical director and I listened in astonishment to what happened next. Instead of hearing the English version of the carol that started the track, we heard the Polish version! It was technically impossible, but that was what we were hearing. As I was to learn later, that was not the only impossible thing that happened during that program.

Two days after the holiday music program aired, I received a call from a young man who insisted on seeing me. "Not a chance," I replied. "It's too close to Christmas and I am much too busy." He quickly changed my mind, however, when he told me that it was he who had called to request repeated playings of "Hush-a-Bye," and that he had a story he wanted to share with me.

We met just a few hours later. He grasped my hand and shook it so hard and so long I thought he'd never stop. His rapid speech was broken only by the tears that streamed down his face and the frequent blowing of his nose. This is his story:

His name is Walter, and he is of Polish descent. His mother, Clara, whom he loved dearly, had suffered a massive stroke that left her paralyzed and unconscious. She surprised the doctors by living ten days in that condition when the expert opinion was that death was only a few hours away. Walter and his wife had been by her bedside at the hospital, prepared for the end, but praying for a miracle.

The night of my radio show, shortly after ten P.M., the strains of a familiar carol drifted into her hospital room. The music annoyed Walter at first. His mother was dying; who wants to hear Christmas carols at a time like that? It must be coming from the room across the hall, he thought, shaking his head in annoyance. Some people just have no consideration!

"Look, Walter," his wife said then, "look at your mother." Clara's head seemed to shake slightly. Her lips twitched. Thinking death had arrived, Walter ran to the nurses' station for help.

The nurse summoned a doctor, but by the time the doctor arrived, Clara seemed as before. Silent and unmoving, comatose. The doctor had no explanation for the head movement or the twitching lips and left soon after reading the monitor.

It was Walter's wife who believed the music had something to do with Clara's slight response. "Call the station, Walter," she suggested. "Ask them to play the song again." And Walter did. By the time he returned to the room after making the phone call, we were already playing the music he'd requested. As he watched with his wife and the nurse, all three were stunned as Clara—a woman paralyzed for ten days—moved her head a full three or four inches, her jaw and bottom lip trembling as if . . . as if she were trying to sing the song. Walter needed no coaching. Half crying, half singing, he stood at his mother's bedside and sang, *"Lulajże Jezuniu, lulajże lulai, a ty go matuniu u płaczu u tulaj."*

As Walter tells it, even in her eighties his mother had still insisted on attending midnight mass every Christmas. And her main reason was to sing "Hush-a-Bye Wee Jesus," her favorite carol. She wanted to sing it to the baby Jesus, just as she had sung it every night to her baby Walter.

You can imagine what happened next. Within hours his mother was awake and singing with anyone who would join her. Clara left the hospital about a week later. As for the music—well, no one has really figured it out yet. Walter thought the music was coming from across the hall, but it couldn't have been. You see, there are no radios on that floor of the hospital, and no intercom system that pipes in music. Could someone have been carrying a boom box walking down the hall? No, those radios aren't allowed there, either. And if someone had been sneaking around with one, Walter or the nurse would have spotted them, either when the nurse came into the room or when Walter went to use the phone to call the station. And why would the person with the forbidden radio have stopped just outside of Clara's room?

I suppose the mystery will never really be solved, and maybe the details aren't important anyway. For me, it's enough to believe that perhaps somebody upstairs with the power to override all the hospital rules understood how important music is to the healing process, and just wanted to hear Clara sing "Hush-a-Bye Wee Jesus" to Him one more time.

FRANK BARANOWSKI
Phoenix, Arizona

Paul and the Puppies

I GREW UP around lots of animals and dreamed that I would continue to own pets when I got married and had my own family. I married a seminary student, however, and it took both our incomes just for the bare necessities. In seven years we had three sons, whose combined energy left me exhausted most of the time. Even though I still wanted pets, when I started noticing that even my houseplants were dying from neglect, I knew I couldn't handle one more living creature whose survival would depend on me.

But the desire for a pet still nagged at me. Maybe it was because I yearned to have someone in my life who would obey me without talking back. As hard as I tried to set rules and consistently follow through with the boys, their rambunctious antics usually got the best of me. Getting them to obey was a bigger challenge than I had ever expected; I was outnumbered and overwhelmed. I was losing control. But a pet—a dog—perhaps would obey me. I knew how to train animals, and besides, I reasoned, a dog would surely help tame the boys.

I shared my ideas with Jimmy, my husband and head of our family. He said flatly, "No. We are not getting a dog." So, instead of trying to convince him, I quietly took my desire to the Lord in prayer, and waited. One day as I was driving into town, I saw some movement in the grass beside the road. I pulled the car over and got out to investigate. It was a puppy! I looked about for the owner but saw no one—there weren't even any houses nearby. Feeling as though I had experienced a miracle from God, I joyously scooped the puppy into my arms. Then suddenly I saw another one! I ran toward the second puppy and then discovered several more down an embankment. A whole litter of puppies, and I was there to save them—I was ecstatic!

I rushed them to the vet to be checked. They were all perfectly healthy. I drove them directly to Jimmy's office at the church and told him to come out and look in the car to see what God had provided for our family. On the way out to the car I tried to soften the blow by telling him about my secret prayer.

He took one look at those seven puppies and then looked back at me as though I had lost my mind.

"Lucy! We cannot possibly keep them! You must take them back to the side of the road and leave them."

I wanted to respect my husband's wishes, but I couldn't bring myself to put these sweet puppies in danger. So I drove back to the area where I had discovered them, found the nearest group of houses, and began knocking on doors. I came to an old rundown shack next to a cornfield. I took a deep breath, mustered my courage, and stepped up on the porch. An old man came to the door and said, "Those are my puppies. I can't understand how they got out. Wait just a minute." He walked over to a table, got his wallet, and counted out ten dollars. "Here's something for your trouble," he said, and handed me the bills through the open screen door. It was a convincing gesture of ownership, but I didn't want to take money for reuniting the puppies with their owner, so I thanked him, assured him the puppies were in good health according to the vet, and left empty-handed.

Months went by and I still had a dog on my mind. Just before Christmas a woman from church called and said, "I've been racking my brain trying to come up with a special gift for Jimmy. He's done so many wonderful things for our family that I'd like to show our appreciation. I decided that I want to give him one of our puppies, but I thought I'd better check with you to make sure you wouldn't object."

Now, how could I ever stifle such a spirit of giving? I assured her that a puppy would be an appropriate expression of love and asked if it would be possible to bring it over Christmas Eve night.

"My family will be here then, and it would be a wonderful surprise for all of them. They all love animals." The woman agreed to deliver her six-week-old, registered golden retriever on the appointed night.

In the days that followed, I studied in secret about the breed and learned that it was an excellent family dog. In fact, the golden retriever was the only breed recommended by the

American Pediatric Association because of its consistently gentle nature. I wondered if my prayers for a friendly, obedient dog were finally being answered.

Christmas Eve arrived and seventeen members of my family were all together, laughing and talking, when the doorbell rang. I could hardly contain my excitement as I followed Jimmy to the door. There before us was that wonderful family from church, holding an adorable puppy with a red ribbon around its neck. When they proudly presented their gift to Jimmy, he awkwardly took it and tried to appear more grateful than he was. He bent down and kissed it on the forehead. But then, what else could he do?

The whole family immediately took to our new pet. We named her Noel's Golden Nugget. She was perfect for our active boys, and she loved their energetic attention. But the best part was that I was able to train Nugget, as she actually obeyed me. I even entered her in a dog show, and she won first place. We eventually bred her, had four litters, and sold puppies for years. Jimmy happily tolerated the extra work the dogs created for me, and more than tolerated the extra money they brought in.

At one point I took a picture of three puppies with our middle son, Paul, and entered the picture in a photo contest. Remarkably, it won first place. The *Clarion-Ledger* published it and paid me for it. The newspaper then selected the photo for international competition, and it won an honorable mention. I won more money, and the picture was put on exhibit in New York. Kodak asked for the rights to the photo to use for commercial purposes, and I signed the release. We began to get phone calls from people all over the country saying they thought they had seen a picture of Paul and the puppies in their local stores. Our family was blessed over and over again by the warm response this photo evoked in so many people. The world that had been opened up to our family because of one simple and inspired gift—our Nugget—was beyond my wildest dreams. It was a miracle.

Twelve years later we moved a thousand miles away to Michigan, and I was terribly homesick for my big family back home. One day I opened the Kroger supplement in the newspaper to check out the weekly specials. There it was again: that same picture of Paul and the puppies, advertising Kodak film. Somehow, seeing that picture in my new town gave me a welcome feeling and the conviction that everything would be all right there.

I've always been amused that "dog" is "God" spelled backward. In our case, there was a definite connection, and we have been equally blessed by both.

LUCY WHITSETT MCGUIRE
Novi, Michigan

The Search for Mary

VERYTHING WAS READY for the most wonderful time of the year. After weeks of preparation, golden reindeer and sleigh nestled on the mantel amid fresh-cut greens enhanced by dozens of glittering lights. Santas graced the piano, while garlands and ribbons adorned the stairway.

The Christmas tree was lovely, laden with precious ornaments collected over many years, and tiny red lights twinkled among the soft branches. Under the fragrant tree, piles of gaily wrapped gifts awaited the eager fingers of children. The house was filled with the delicious aroma of homemade cookies and candies and the heady scent of pine and fir.

But one thing was missing: The mystery, the miracle, and the wonder of the spirit of Christmas had not entered into my heart. A wise person once said that miracles are for believers and that miracles are the soul of Christmas, which is love. If we have the spirit, we know it, but when it eludes us, we hunger and long for it.

My one hope lay in the ceramic Nativity set I had been working on for months. It was in its final firing and would be ready by six P.M. the day before Christmas Eve, and I could not be late. That day had now arrived. I thought that maybe, when the beautiful, creamy-white pieces were in place in our bay window, the Christmas spirit also would arrive.

A blinding snow and ice storm raged outside with biting, slashing wind, and darkness was settling in earlier than usual. It was already past five o'clock, and my eighteen-year-old son and I were just leaving to brave the slippery drive to the ceramic shop when the phone rang. The voice on the other end of the line sounded feeble and desperate.

"This is Alice, your neighbor," the quavering voice whispered. "I dropped a glass of water in the kitchen, and the glass broke and I cannot see to clean it up. Please help me."

Alice was the elderly lady living next door. She was almost blind and deaf, and unable to get around without a walker since fracturing her hip. At that moment I did not want to help her, but since she used that most powerful word, "neighbor," I had no choice.

The mess in her kitchen was worse than I expected. The glass had shattered, and shards and splinters were everywhere. While I crawled on my hands and knees mopping up the water and picking up pieces of glass, I could feel Alice squinting at me through her thick lenses as she stood nearby clutching her walker with severely crippled arthritic hands that had once glided effortlessly, magically, over piano and organ keys, bringing untold delight and joy to many. Her feet and ankles were swollen and misshapen now; yet once she had danced.

She was well over ninety years old, childless and widowed, but still proud and intelligent. It must have hurt her to call for help.

When I left her, only ten minutes remained before the deadline at the ceramic shop. Luckily, there were only a few other drivers braving the storm. A block from our destination, we saw a station wagon stalled by the side of the road, distress lights flashing, and a girl standing in the snow, frantically waving for help as we inched past her.

Then my son shouted, "I know that girl! We must help her!" Before I could protest, he was out of our car and at her side, returning in a few minutes to explain that the car was out of gas, and that he would drop me off at the ceramic shop and return for me as soon as he helped his friend get on her way again.

It was after six when I reached the shop, and the shade was drawn on the entry door with a CLOSED sign attached. I pounded on the glass with frozen fingers.

There was a faint light visible around the shade, and finally the owner peeked out. Her face was angry and her voice cold as she reminded me that I was late. Then she closed the door as I waited in the snow and wind for her to slide two large boxes down the step into the parking lot.

When we reached home we started unpacking the pieces carefully. They were so lovely, so smooth, so creamy white. Gently we placed them in the bay window in the dining room. First the shepherds and sheep, followed by the oxen and the donkey, the wise men and camels, and the angel that would hover over all.

Last, we set out the holy family. There was Joseph and then the child and his little manger. But where was Mary? In disbelief we checked each piece again, shaking out the shredded packing material, scattering it on the carpet. The second-most-important piece was not there.

With a sinking heart, I called the ceramic shop, listening to the ringing and ringing. She had to be there! Finally she answered in a weary voice.

"Mary is not here," I said.

"She has to be," the exhausted voice replied. "Look again."

"I did, I did," I insisted. "She is not there."

"Wait," she said. After what seemed like a long time, I heard her say with great sadness and dismay, "Missed her somehow when I fired the others. I will have her ready the day after Christmas. Come back then."

She hung up the phone, and even though I dialed over and over, there was nothing but the ringing.

The next day was Christmas Eve. The snow was still coming down, so I left home a little earlier for my job as a nurse at the long-term-care facility a mile away. I knew some of our staff members would call to say they couldn't come in because of the bad weather and the holiday bus schedule, and others would just not come.

As expected, there were fewer workers than usual to care for more than one hundred patients. All of us worked as a team, feeding, turning, lifting, and bathing. We helped cook, wash and fold laundry, mop floors, anything that needed doing.

All the women were dressed in their prettiest clothes, their hair combed and curled, makeup applied to wrinkled faces. All the men were nicely dressed and cleanly shaven.

We sang Christmas songs to them, songs from their childhood. Some joined in ever so sweetly. Most of all, we comforted them. We talked to and touched each person. We listened to their Christmas memories, to their losses. When the shift ended we clocked out, but some of us stayed to make sure everyone would be served a nourishing meal and be put to bed on clean sheets when it was time.

By the time I left to go home, the snow had stopped and the wind was gentle. The world seemed clean and soft in the pristine silence. It was transformed into a beautiful wonderland, its rough edges smooth, its scars and wounds hidden.

It was very cold and clear, the kind of night that made countless stars visible. I wondered if the shepherds had seen these same stars that first Christmas.

The miracle of Christmas comes when least expected. The wonder, the awe, and the mystery come silently when there is room at the inn in our hearts, when our wants and deepest longings are put aside to embrace the needs and longings of others:

"This is Alice, your neighbor," the feeble voice had entreated.

"I know that girl! We must help!" said our caring child.

"I missed her somehow," the craft-shop owner had said with sadness.

All of these were viewed as obstacles, as stumbling blocks,

when in reality they were guideposts leading me to Bethlehem, to the miracle of Christmas.

When I was a little girl, an old nun who taught us religion told us to keep our eyes on the star, not only at Christmas but all our lives, and we would never lose our way. In the hustle and bustle of preparing for Christmas, it is easy to lose our way, to lose sight of the star and miss the miracle.

Later that evening, while my family and I listened to carols, the peace and quiet were interrupted by the ringing of the doorbell. We were not expecting anyone and wondered who would be out in the cold on Christmas Eve.

I opened the door, and in the darkness I saw the owner of the ceramic shop, still wearing her paint-spattered apron. Her face was lined with exhaustion and a kind of radiance and her eyes were filled with joy and light. We looked at each other, two believers who had found the miracle of Christmas.

In her hands, partly concealed by an old rag, was Mary: perfect, beautiful, creamy white. In silence she handed Mary to me, our hands touching for a moment.

"Merry Christmas," she whispered as she vanished into the starry night.

HELEN KINZELER
Oakwood, Ohio

Running on Instinct

I HAD ALREADY had three children, so with my last pregnancy I just knew something was different. Something was wrong. Out shopping with my sister one day, we stopped to look at a display of tiny infant booties and socks. And I suddenly knew what it was that was wrong.

"Don't bother buying any socks. This baby doesn't have any feet," I announced, standing there in the aisle.

My sister looked at me, startled. "What on earth are you saying, Reda? How do you know the baby doesn't have any feet?"

"He never kicks. All of my other babies kicked, and this one never does." I truly believed that the baby I was carrying didn't have feet. But the thought never really made me feel sad. If that was God's plan, if that was the way it was, I would deal with it.

It sounds so crazy now, of course, to carry a baby for nine months not knowing if it would be born with feet. This was long before the days of ultrasound, long before expectant moms could get an early peek at what was growing inside of them. Back then, the first glimpse of your newborn baby was in the delivery room, when you were groggy from the anesthetic.

I shared my thoughts with my doctor, too. He smiled sadly and shook his head at my announcement. In his eyes I was just another anxious pregnant woman. His expression was different some months later, though, when I woke up from being sedated during the baby's delivery.

"What's wrong?" I asked immediately.

"Well," he said, looking down at me as I lay there in the hospital bed, "you were right."

My first question startled him. "Does he have feet at all?" I wanted to know.

"Yes, he does have feet, but they are severely deformed."

Strange as it may sound, I was not upset. If he didn't have feet at all, then it was out of my hands entirely. But if he had feet, I knew he would someday walk. I was certain of it.

My little baby Chris's feet were not a pretty sight. Lifeless and green from lack of blood flow, they were also turned one hundred and eighty degrees in the wrong direction. His feet were just dangling there, hanging from the rest of his body. The nurses were so concerned that the sight of his feet would upset the other new mothers in the ward that they drew the curtains around my bed whenever they brought him to me.

The doctors told my husband and me that our son

Chris's chances of ever walking were slim unless he underwent a series of five painful surgeries. The day after he was born his feet were broken and cast, and then adjusted and recast every six weeks for six months. At six months he was fitted with orthopedic shoes and braces, to continue the process of turning his feet around to point in the proper direction.

It was a hard time for us. It broke our hearts to see a small infant in so much pain from the constant manipulation of his feet—sometimes he was blue in the face from holding his breath because of the crying.

By the time Chris was nine months old, I had had enough of my baby's painful wails. I would wait in the mornings until my husband, James, went off to work and the older children had left for school. Then I would take Chris's braces off and rub his feet in my hands to comfort him. I knew that I was defying the doctor's orders, but I felt that as his mother, I needed to do all that I could to help my son. Something instinctively told me that massaging his little deformed feet would be helpful. I would bend over his feet and rub them, and I would talk to his feet, too, trying to make them straighten out. And I would think to myself, *God, if you let my son walk, I promise to give you all of the credit. I won't take any for myself.* Late in the afternoon, when the rest of the family was due home, I would grit my teeth and put Chris's braces back on so they wouldn't know what I was up to. I hated listening to him whimper in pain as I'd tighten the straps every day.

One day after everyone else had left the house and I'd

removed the braces, an extraordinary thing happened. As I watched in amazement, my little nine-month-old son pulled himself up by grabbing the side of the couch. Most babies his age could do that, of course, but he'd never done it before. What he did next was even more amazing. He walked! Not only did he walk, he ran! I rushed him to the doctor, the same doctor who had given me the grim news so many months before. He watched in surprise as Chris flip-flopped across the floor of the examining room. "This is amazing, Mrs. Wallace," he said quietly. "This is a miracle."

Chris has never really stopped running since. Sure, he was a bit clumsy, and his gait was awkward, but it was clear early on that Chris had real athletic talent. Over the years his talent has grown—first with T-ball, then with Little League, and with a record-breaking football career in high school. And I am proud to say that his athletic career did not end with high school graduation.

My son Chris, the baby who I thought did not have any feet, the baby whom the doctors told us might never walk at all, is the star quarterback at the University of Toledo. In his first year he tore through the record books and eclipsed a total of nine school records. He runs on the edges of his feet, and he goes through sports shoes like peanuts. His running style has been described as a cross between a penguin and a pigeon. But when I watch my son run down that field, with the ball tucked under his arm and a crowd of big men chasing him, I remember how I felt so many years ago—how I knew that, if he had feet, those feet would work.

From the day my baby was born, I knew in my heart he

would walk. No one ever could've convinced me otherwise. With Chris's little feet in my hands, I believed all God was asking me was to take care of the possible—and to trust Him with the impossible. And that's exactly what I did.

REDA WALLACE
Springfield, Ohio

The Birth of a Father

THERE ARE MOMENTS in your life when your mind takes a picture. A snapshot to remember—an image so special, so poignant, that you lock it away in the photo album of your memory, to be looked at over and over again, savored for years to come.

This is especially true for mothers. Watching babies develop and children grow is perhaps one of life's greatest joys, a time when many precious memories are made and stored. Sometimes during her busy day-to-day routine, however, a mother forgets to stop and enjoy the moment, not realizing that memories are being made even amidst the most mundane events in life. And then later, when her world slows down and the children are gone, that mother finds herself aching to turn back the pages in her mind—trying to recapture that special feeling of love and connectedness that exists between a mother and her young children.

As the mother of four children, I have collected many of those treasured pictures. One of these early memories was triggered recently while watching my grown son prepare for the birth of his first child. The night his wife went into labor I could see the nervousness on his face. It was obvious his emotions were mixed—the uncertainty of what was about to happen, anticipation, joy, fear—wondering if he would remember everything he had to do to help his wife through this important moment in their lives.

Watching him that night took me back to a day sixteen years before, when my son was six years old. We had a female cat at the time who was ready to give birth to kittens. Like all young children, Andre was curious and excited to see the birth of these new babies. I felt he was old enough to view the miraculous event, so I answered his questions and prepared him as much as possible so he wouldn't be shocked or scared.

My young son decided to prepare a special box for the mother cat, whom he affectionately called "Mindy." Like a mother-to-be out shopping for bibs and cribs, Andre went from store to store with his older brother to find just the right cardboard box for the special event. He finally found a box he felt would be appropriate—low enough for Mindy to get in and out of when she wanted to eat, but not so low that the kittens could climb out when they became more active. He put a warm blanket on the bottom of the box, cut a square piece from the side for Mindy's "door," and placed a small stuffed toy in the corner "so the first new kitten wouldn't be lonely while waiting for the arrival of his next brother or sister."

Finally he stood back and admired his handiwork. Feeling satisfied with the job, he introduced Mindy to her new sleeping quarters. A big smile of pride and contentment came across his face when the cat curled up in the corner and began to purr, obviously pleased with her new cozy birthing center.

The day the blessed event took place, one kitten had been born by the time Andre arrived home from school. He was thrilled and amazed with what he saw. He would lay his hand on the mother cat's belly and feel the other kittens moving and waiting their turn to be born. He talked softly to Mindy while he stroked her, trying to reassure her that he was close by. When Mindy began to yowl very loudly, it was clear the second kitten was on its way.

When the second kitten was born and the mother was busy taking care of it and preparing for the next, he asked, "Mommy, how come she cries so loud when the baby comes?" In my delight at having a son interested in this amazing process, despite thinking I had prepared him for it, I had not thought to explain about the pain of giving birth. Not wanting to detract from what he was witnessing, I tried to explain that it was not hurtful pain but a pain of great pleasure for the mother cat, knowing her babies would soon be born.

Andre continued to watch Mindy intently, praising her and complimenting her for doing such a good job. With the birth of the next kitten he suddenly turned to me and said, "Mommy, I know why the kittens come out that end." Trying to keep a straight face as I imagined what was coming, I asked him why he thought that was. "Because the other end has teeth," he said matter-of-factly. I thought I would die laughing inside, but at the same time marveled at the logic of his observation.

When the impending birth of the next kitten was obvious by the cries of the mother, I glanced at Andre to offer words of comfort, in case the ordeal was becoming too stressful for him. I saw tears rolling down his cheeks. When I asked him why he was crying, he looked up at me with his big, soulful eyes and said, "Mommy, I'm sorry I gave you all that pain to have me."

I thought my heart would burst with love. Holding him close, I reassured him that his birth had done nothing but bring smiles to my life, and that the pain of having a baby meant very little compared with the joy of having him for a son. He gave me a big hug and then quickly turned his attention back to Mindy and the arrival of another tiny kitten. He watched eagerly as each one came. Finally, our dear mother cat was finished and exhausted, but had six beautiful babies to show for all her hard work.

Now, sixteen years later, Andre was hugging me again after witnessing an even more amazing birth process. As he put his strong arms around me and whispered, "Love you, Mom," I felt the same love I had felt many years before. I knew by the proud look in his eyes that he had succeeded in helping his wife with the delivery of their new baby boy, just as he had helped encourage Mindy's delivery years before. Tears came to my eyes as I thought about him being there with his wife, stroking her gently, wiping her brow, offering words of comfort when she cried out in pain.

Only this time, I knew Andre wouldn't be questioning why a mother cries out when she brings a new baby into the world. This time, I knew he would understand.

DEBBIE MCLELLAN
New Brunswick, Canada

Showers of Blessing

HERE WASN'T A cloud in the sky that warm June morning when my friend Carole and I set off for a day of shopping. We had learned of a quaint quilt shop, nestled deep in the Appalachian Mountains, that showcased the wares of nearby artisans. Carole's heart was set on finding a blue-and-white Dresden plate quilt to put the finishing touch on her guest bedroom.

We parked the car next to the only traffic light in town, and, armed with fabric swatches and paint chips, we scurried across the street. Next door to the quilt shop, however, we spotted a ladies' boutique and were lured inside. Delighting in the pleasure of the unexpected, Carole perused the handbags while I admired the most exquisite collection of rainwear I'd ever seen. I ran my fingers across a vinyl-laminated floral chintz umbrella and exclaimed: "These are the most gorgeous umbrellas . . . Why, they're just like an old-fashioned flower garden."

A salesclerk hastened to my side. "Perhaps you'd like to try one of them out," she suggested. "Unless, of course, you're leery about opening an umbrella indoors."

"An umbrella this lovely certainly couldn't bring bad luck," I mused, remembering the ridiculous superstition. Impulsively, I opened the oversized canopy. Underneath its protective bouquet, I felt wonderfully carefree and sheltered from the whole world.

But with graduate-school tuition and new tires to buy, today I had no money for expensive umbrellas. Besides, even if I could afford one, it wouldn't be a practical purchase.

Back in the sixth grade, I'd once eyed a beautiful, pink frilly umbrella in a department-store window. "Safety patrols need nice umbrellas," I'd explained to Mother.

"Safety patrols need serviceable umbrellas, not flimsy parasols," she'd countered. "Besides, you might lose it."

Everything our family owned, it seemed, was serviceable: my brother's no-nonsense gray coat, my twin sister's saddle oxfords, and those drab grosgrain ribbons I wore on my pigtails. How I'd wanted to own something pretty as well as practical.

But even as an adult, I'd continued to settle for plain-Jane umbrellas. My collapsible umbrella, a peculiar shade of navy blue, fit neatly in the pocket of my briefcase. It was of the should-go-great-with-everything-but-never-quite-matches-anything variety. Practical and serviceable but, unfortunately, I never lost it.

"Thanks for showing me the umbrella," I wistfully muttered to the boutique clerk, and headed next door to the quilt shop, a few steps ahead of Carole.

When my friend's steps caught up with mine, I noticed a long, slender box under her arm. "This is for you," she said softly. "I've never seen you look so longingly at anything before."

"But, Carole, it's not Christmas. It's not even my birthday," I protested as I opened the box. "And you were going to buy a quilt today."

"Look, there won't always be sunshine in the sky like today," she answered convincingly. "And when the rain comes, I want you to think happy thoughts of friendship." I was speechless and deeply touched.

Once we were inside the quilt shop, the manager told Carole: "I just sold the last Dresden plate quilt and we won't have any more until next spring. Our quilters can corn and beans during the summer months, you know."

Carole paused briefly to examine Log Cabin and Star of Bethlehem designs, but none was the right shade of blue. "That's okay. I can always buy a quilt another time," she insisted, with not a hint of disappointment in her voice.

I tossed the umbrella's box in the backseat of the car and placed my treasure beside me for the long drive home. It smelled like a brand-new toy, and I felt as cared for as a little girl tucked in bed with her teddy bear. I rolled down the car window, shut my eyes, and inhaled the pure mountain air. My thoughts wandered to another time and place, and to other lovely umbrellas. On an October evening twelve years before, my wedding attendants had carried Victorian lace parasols. "When the storms of life fall upon this couple, as surely they fall upon us all," the minister had prayed, "please be their shelter and their refuge."

I didn't understand it, but in the weeks that followed, I found myself thinking a lot about umbrellas. I couldn't pass a store display without lingering for a second look. Suddenly I noticed all the broken, frayed, and faded umbrellas people all around me carried. Sometimes, warm and dry inside my car during a storm, I'd see folks with no umbrella at all. When I spotted a lady dashing to her car with a plastic bag over the top of her head and an elderly man wrestling with umbrella spokes that refused to cooperate, it was as if God was saying to me: "Why not start an umbrella ministry? You just give the umbrellas away and trust Me to do the rest."

I found the idea strangely appealing. I'd become so busy writing lately that I didn't have time to sew or bake much anymore and I'd really missed giving special presents to others. Yet stitchery and cookies were safe gifts. Umbrellas were, well, a bit strange.

"You want me to give away umbrellas?" I asked God one day. "What if someone thinks that I am the one who doesn't have sense enough to come in out of the rain?"

Coincidentally, at about that time my comfortable office at work was temporarily moved outdoors to a trailer with no canopied breezeway. During rainstorms, water collected on the roof and poured down in torrents as I came and went, dampening me despite the oversized umbrella Carole had given to me. I began to think incessantly about umbrellas.

Cautiously, to test the waters (so to speak) of this new venture, I purchased only one umbrella at a time. First, I gave an umbrella to an acquaintance who was facing surgery. "Into each life some rain must fall. I hope that sunny days are ahead," I explained. As it turned out, her surgery wasn't successful and I felt utterly foolish. Then she sent me this note: "Thanks for that beautiful umbrella. I can't explain it, but each time I look at it, I feel so loved."

Soon after, a friend whose son had left home telephoned. "Could you just come and spend the evening with me?" she asked. I took her an umbrella, and without saying a word, I prayed that God's "Son"shine would touch her home and shield her from the storms.

As time went on, I discovered wonderful umbrellas on sale at record low prices. I discreetly stashed some in a hallway closet and tucked others in a sack in the backseat of my car. "Please show people that You are the real source of the umbrellas," I prayed. And, with few words exchanged, the recipients amazingly understood that the umbrellas symbolized both friendship and God's blanket of protection.

It had seemed at first to be the kind of undertaking I could keep hidden, camouflaged in the secret corners of my heart, my closet, and my car. I chose my umbrella recipients with precision—people whose paths never crossed; out-of-towners; total strangers; a colleague who had lost her job; a friend who moved to a new city; a high school graduate; an innkeeper who operates a bed-and-breakfast establishment; a farmer selling tomatoes at a roadside stand; friends facing a monsoon of difficulty and passersby who seemed to need a bit of encouragement.

But one day a neighbor dropped by unannounced during fall cleaning and blew my cover.

"What in the world are you doing with all these umbrellas?" she asked in astonishment, giving me a do-we-have-a-fixation-with-umbrellas stare. I offered a lame explanation as she pulled two umbrellas—a delicate child's parasol and an executive paisley model—from an overflowing shopping bag.

Hearing the commotion, my husband rushed to the scene. "Can you believe this?" he chided. "My wife who talks nonstop during the weather report is giving away umbrellas!" I had even kept my secret from my husband, fearing he would think me crazy!

But to my surprise, he knelt excitedly by the shopping bag. "I haven't had a new umbrella myself in years," he exclaimed. "Can I trade in my old, scruffy one? Here, this one matches my truck."

A few days later I took an umbrella to a shut-in friend who was seriously ill with heart disease. The design on this one was a reproduction of newspaper print in black-and-white—very appropriate because my friend had been a newspaper reporter and writer for many years. She accepted the gift with great happiness while huge tears rolled down both cheeks. "You just don't know what this means to me," she said.

"You really like it?" I asked.

"Oh yes, but more than that it is the hope it gives me,

because obviously you think I'll be able to walk in the rain once more, as well as that I'll be writing again."

Soon after, I happened upon shelves of lovely umbrellas at a nearby glassware outlet. "I have a feeling you're the umbrella lady," the manager quipped with a curious glance at my armful of finds. "I've heard of you, and do I have a deal for you! If you buy one umbrella, I'll give you two for free. The manufacturer got us mixed up with another company and sent us their overstock of umbrellas." I scooped up another one featuring a perky apple motif, sure to charm any teacher.

The following week, a teacher from Arizona telephoned me. "I read your recent article about a teacher in one of the crafts magazines," she explained. "I'll be passing through West Virginia, and I'd like to meet with you."

"What do you think about giving her an umbrella?" I asked a friend. "You know, I just bought one with red apples splattered all over it."

"I wouldn't do it if I were you," she said. "It doesn't seem professional. And, besides, you've never even met her before. She'll think you're crazy."

So, dressed in the "proper" clothes and prepared to say the "proper" words, I drove to the restaurant where we were to meet. As I opened my car door, there came a sudden downpour. After I located the teacher in the lobby, she admitted with a lighthearted laugh: "I know this will sound silly, but I forgot to pack an umbrella. Where I live, we haven't had any rain for weeks."

Swiftly, I felt regret at having no umbrella for her. Why

had I not trusted my instincts? Why had I sought someone else's opinion and allowed another person to put a damper on my umbrella ministry?

That evening, I wrapped the frivolous apple-print umbrella in practical plain brown paper, tied it up with a piece of heavy, serviceable twine, and addressed it to my new friend. I was certain that she, too, could use something pretty as well as practical.

"Another umbrella?" the postmistress queried with a wink the next morning. By now she was familiar with the contents of my ubiquitous long, slender boxes. "This one's bound for Arizona," she said, chuckling, as the relentless rain poured outside. "An umbrella headed for the desert; now, that's a new one."

I smiled to myself at the wonder of how an umbrella—such a simple object—when received unexpectedly can brighten just about anyone's day and can help people from all walks of life to feel cared for and protected. I dashed to my car, sheltered by the umbrella Carole had given to me on a cloudless day more that a year earlier. The purchase no longer seemed like a spur-of-the-moment shopping whim, but a moment orchestrated by God Himself. And it taught me a valuable lesson. Never again, I promised myself, would I allow anyone to squelch an inner prompting to reach out to someone else, no matter how trivial it seemed. This time it had been a compelling urge to give away umbrellas, but in the future there would be other ideas, other opportunities, and I must never disregard them. The opinions of others no longer seemed important.

When I tuned in the car radio, I heard the weatherman's grim prediction: "More rain expected tomorrow, for the third day in a row."

But I've been growing rather fond of precipitation. For hidden deep in my heart is God's bright forecast: "Continued showers of blessing."

VICTORIA HANSEN
Charlotte, North Carolina

The Family Across the Way

WHEN I WAS just starting out in life, I rented a one-bedroom apartment in a cheap complex full of college kids and other young roommates. The one exception was the young family that lived across from me in an apartment not much bigger than mine. Our windows faced each other. Neither of us could afford drapes.

I was busy working at night and taking classes at the local community college during the day. My family was still a little upset about my dropping out of the more prestigious state university I'd originally been attending, and I was still feeling guilty about wasting all of their money. We weren't exactly burning up the phone lines trying to call each other.

And so I did a bit of vicarious living by observing the family across the way. They were a modern version of the Waltons. The kid was always drawing at the kitchen table with a glass of milk and a plate of cookies not far out of reach. The mom sat around with some sewing she took in, and around five o'clock each evening the dad came in and tossed his thin jacket on the coatrack. Mother and son jumped up from whatever they were doing and hugged him as if he'd been gone for days instead of hours. I watched the same sweet scene unfold five days a week. If I hadn't seen it with my own eyes, I wouldn't have believed it either.

During the week before Christmas, I made a quick trip home to visit my family. I had just started a new job, and as the new guy I was scheduled to work straight through the holidays, so I had to make my visit short. We opened a few gifts, hugged a lot, mended a family fence or two, and after two days I was right back "home" in my crummy little apartment.

On my first day back I glanced through the window at the family across the way, and noticed that things looked . . . different. The kid was at the table, but there was no glass of milk. No plate of cookies. The mom was sewing, but she could barely hold her head up. Five o'clock came. Five o'clock went. No dad. No jacket on the flimsy coatrack. I waited to leave for my evening restaurant shift until the very last minute. By five-fifty there was still no sign of Dad.

I walked past their front door on my way to work, and my heart sank at what I saw: Large and round on their front door hung a fresh funeral wreath. I cried on the way to work, as if the man had been my own father. Their picture-perfect family had given me hope that such happiness actually existed in the world. Now, with their lives shattered, my optimistic fantasies gave way to a deep sense of despair. I thought of their cheap apartment and cramped living space and wondered how they would ever manage without him. The ghostly sound of their old laughter rang through my ears all night.

On the way home I wondered how I could help. I was afraid of causing them more pain if I offered condolences, and who was I to them, anyway? What would they think if some college punk growing a skinny goatee and wearing a tip apron knocked on their door and admitted that he'd been substituting their warm, loving family life for the lack of his, the past six months?

Days passed, and the family across the way grew more pitiful by the hour. They sat. They stood. They came in and out of focus, yet nothing changed. Their grief could be felt all the way over on my side of our green-and-tan building. Carols rang out over my radio and garish red-and-green cartoons splashed across the TV, and for the first time in my life I realized what was meant by the term "the holiday blues." If I felt that sad, I could only imagine how they must've been feeling.

That's it! I thought as I threw on my uniform for my Christmas Eve shift. The family across the way hadn't hung a single string of tinsel or a measly bough of holly. Why, it didn't look as though they'd even turned on a single light since the father had passed away. Maybe a Christmas tree would help cheer them up.

I bustled through work, overflowing with false holiday cheer and pushing my good graces to the limit all night so that my tables would be generous with the holiday tips. It worked and I sped off after my shift to scout the late-night tree lots.

Unfortunately, such things only existed in cheesy holiday specials on TV's Family Channel. All the tree stands were closed, and even the twenty-four-hour megastores were out of the fake variety. I cursed myself for waiting until the last minute to do something nice for those two lost souls across the way, then pulled into a gas station on the way home. The least I could do was bring them a CARE package of milk and Christmas cookies for the little kid.

The wizened old lady behind the counter sucked on cigarettes and watched carefully as I loaded a little red basket with cold cuts and orange juice, candy canes and eggnog. I made my way to the counter and spotted a tabletop tree beside the cash register.

"Is your tree for sale?" I asked around her halo of cigarette smoke.

"It is now," she croaked when she saw the stack of ones and fives in my eager hand. "Thirty bucks," she said without flinching.

"Thirty bucks?" I said. "But . . . it's Christmas Eve!"

"I know," she said, smiling. "You should have heard the price I quoted the last guy who asked me. You're getting a deal."

I bundled up the tree in one of her plastic Stop 'n Go sacks and brought it to my place to try to air the stale smoke smell out of it before I presented it to the family across the way. I plugged the tree lights in to test them and to burn off a little of the nicotine smell. I stacked a plate with cold cuts and cheese, and another with cookies and chocolates, then covered them in Saran Wrap.

Then, just for a second, I sat down in my dilapidated, secondhand easy chair to see how my meager offerings might look to the family across the way.

A knock at the door woke me much, much later. I sprang to my feet, spying the plates of food and brightly blazing tree still sitting on my small dinner table. How long had I been asleep?

I opened the door to find the mother and son from across the way. They looked concerned and they pointed to my tree.

"We saw the tree still burning and you sleeping beside it," they said shyly. "We were worried you'd burn your house down."

I saw the little boy eyeing the chocolate and cookies and quickly invited them in. I sat them down and found a station playing carols on the radio while they ate. I poured eggnog and orange juice and sat down quietly beside them.

I peeked out of my window at their dark and dismal apartment. How bright and alive my tree must have seemed to them as they whiled away the lonely hours of their first Christmas Eve without the man of their family.

And how pitiful I must have looked beside it, asleep in my broken-down chair, all alone on Christmas. How incredible that in the depths of their despair, they could still feel concern . . . for me.

I had been so eager to surprise them. To rush home and get everything ready. To knock on their door and show them that the world was not such a horrible place after all. To offer them a miracle.

But in the end, the little family from across the way rose above their own sorrow and brought the gift of unexpected friendship to me.

RUSTY FISCHER
Greensboro, North Carolina

Comfort My Children

I T WAS TWILIGHT on a cold and rainy October day in 1968, and I was riding my bicycle home from work in Copenhagen, Denmark. My husband was in Canada on an assignment at that time, and I was alone with our two children, our son, age ten, and our daughter, age seven.

On my way home I had to cross a very busy four-lane road with a bicycle lane. For safety, I had made it a habit to get off my bike and walk it across the intersection. On this particular day I got halfway across the street and stopped in the middle to let the cars go by. A small car stopped in the lane to my right, and the driver signaled for me to cross. A big truck stopped in the lane beside the small car, and the truck driver also signaled to me, so I continued across the street. Just as I passed the truck I saw a Volkswagen coming toward me, illegally in the bicycle track, at full speed. There was no time for me to escape, either backward or forward.

In that split second, countless thoughts of my children, my husband, my widowed mother, and my job flashed through my mind, and I prayed more sincerely than ever before, "Please, dear Lord, whatever happens—spare my life."

The car hit the bicycle, slamming the handlebars into the left side of my body. As I lay helpless in the road, I could barely breathe because of the pain, but I didn't lose consciousness. Turning my head, I saw the Volkswagen's tire only an inch away. My bicycle, which had been thrown several feet by the collision, now looked half its original size.

I was certain that I had experienced a miracle. The car tire couldn't have been any closer, yet it had not crushed my head. I felt that an invisible hand had stopped it right there. Tears streamed down my cheeks as I thanked my Heavenly Father for saving my life.

As I lay in the road waiting for the ambulance, I worried about what the children would think when I didn't come for them. Would I be in time to call the day-care center from the emergency room before it closed? Who could I contact? I hardly knew my neighbors because of my busy schedule, and other friends lived some distance away.

At the emergency room, the staff wouldn't allow me to use the telephone before they had taken an X ray. The nurses were too busy to make the call for me and the police officers didn't show up until four hours later to make a written report of the accident.

For the five longest hours of my life I was kept in the hospital with a number of people helping me and working on me. Still, they couldn't do anything about my only real concern—two small and lonely children. All I could do was pray.

"Please tell them I'm all right," I prayed. "Let them have peace of mind so that they won't panic, and give them patience. Please tell them what to do." And as I prayed, an all-embracing peace filled my mind—the same feeling I hoped my children would receive.

Finally, the doctor told me that except for my painfully bruised ribs, I was as good as new, and he let me go. The two policemen offered me a ride home, and we arrived outside my apartment building at ten-fifteen that night.

In the dim light I could see two small, tired children walking hand in hand toward the police car. "Mom, where have you been? What happened to you? How come you're so late? Why did the police drive you home?" they asked as soon as we were safely in the apartment.

I explained and then asked, "How did you get home?"

My son said, "We couldn't understand why you didn't come to pick us up, but we thought you might be late from work, so we walked home. It started to get dark, but we couldn't get in because we didn't have a key.

"I didn't know what to do, but all of a sudden I thought we should pray about it. So we knelt on the doormat while I said a prayer. We sat without talking for a little while after the prayer and then a nice thing happened to me.

"I felt a big, warm hand touching the top of my head, and I heard a friendly voice saying, 'Your mother is well, she has been taken care of. It will be a while before she comes home, and it will be dark outside, but just stay calm. Take your little sister by the hand and stay near the apartment and play peacefully. If you do, the time will go by quickly until your mother is with you again.'

"When I looked up to see who was talking to me, I couldn't see anybody, and no more was said. I just felt calm."

Over the years since that night I have seen my son occasionally struggle as he has grown into adulthood. When things seemed bleakest and he would question even the existence of God, I would gently prod him: "Do you remember what happened to you the night of my accident?"

His features would clear, his eyes would soften, and he would say, "Mother, it's true, what happened to me was true, and I will never be able to deny it."

As with my accident, life's challenges—the inevitable bumps and bruises we experience along the way—can teach us great lessons if we let them. The peace that enveloped my children that night did more than sustain them during those lonely hours away from me. The peace they felt became a source of comfort that would last a lifetime.

METTE HANSEN SCHAER
Salt Lake City, Utah

Finding My Beshert

*L*N 1992 I advertised for a husband in the personal-ads section of a Boston newspaper, *The Jewish Advocate*. After several months of bad dates and no chemistry, I canceled my pitch. "I guess God wants me to meet my future husband some other way," I told myself. Though I held on to my faith that my beshert (soul mate) would eventually show up, I was thirty-three at the time, my biological clock was ticking, and I was scared and impatient. I was also tired of suffering through awkward dates with men who sounded terrific on the telephone and in their letters, but who were a whole different story when encountered in person. I usually wanted to head straight for home—fast.

It turns out that the man of my dreams, my beshert—Stephen—was married at the time my ads were running, and he was not a subscriber to *The Jewish Advocate* anyway. Months later, when Stephen's marriage fell apart, he reluctantly reentered the singles scene. He visited an aunt in another town who gave him her current copy of *The Jewish Advocate*, suggesting that he check out the personal-ads section. When Stephen glanced at the personals column for that week, he saw an ad that immediately grabbed his attention. He wrote to the mystery lady that night. That ad was mine. But how was that possible? I had canceled my ad months earlier. By "coincidence," the newspaper erroneously reentered my ad in the one and only *Jewish Advocate* personals Stephen ever read, long after I had canceled it.

Stephen and I met the night I received his letter. He says he knew on our first date that he wanted to marry me. I felt the same way, but since his divorce wasn't yet final, it took me a few weeks to come to the same conclusion. Stephen warmed up my cold feet in a short time, his divorce was finalized, and we married a year after we met.

I called *The Jewish Advocate* to tell them of our good news and to ask how my ad had ended up back in the newspaper—without my knowledge or permission—months after I had canceled it. I had assumed that they were having a slow month and had put in some old ads just to fill out the classified section. What I heard instead gave me chills. Courtney, the employee who entered the personals each week, knew immediately who I was. She said, "I remember you calling me and specifically telling me to rerun your ad on Labor Day weekend."

"I never called you," I said in amazement. "It must have been my guardian angel."

It's lucky that I didn't settle for one of the "Mr. Wrongs" the week I placed my personals ad in January 1992, because the man I was supposed to marry wasn't available until much later in the year. We needed a "mistake" to bring us together when the time was right for both of us. I believe that our guardian angels orchestrated that mistake.

My flexibility had to extend even further, though, than accepting a delay in my personal time line. Before I met Stephen, I had a clear idea of what I desired in a mate, as well as what I didn't want. I made a list of what I hoped for as well as what I wanted to avoid, just to make sure God had it straight. But God must have thought I needed a lesson in tolerance, because while I did get most of what was on my "wish" list, I also received, in Stephen, most of what was on my "to avoid" list.

I had told God I was a Reform Jew, not interested in a seriously religious man. He sent me a man who was practically an Orthodox Jew. I told God I wanted nothing to do with keeping a kosher home—a practice I considered akin to having an eating disorder. God not only sent me a kosher man but a vegetarian to boot. And I vehemently told God I wasn't interested in raising another woman's children. So God gave me the opportunity to stepparent two adolescent boys, Dov and Otom, who would be living with us full-time.

I believe that Stephen and I could only have found each other through such a miraculous event. If I had received his letter months before, when I was receiving piles of them, I probably would have dumped it in the wastebasket, because of his lack of all the right qualifications. Because I believe that God, in His wisdom, often has plans for me that are different from my own, I can see His hand in the events that brought us together. When Stephen's letter so unexpectedly arrived in my mailbox, I was curious and I paid attention. When I learned how this mistake had occurred, I accepted it as a kind of divine intervention and I became less demanding about my "undesirable" list. After all, who was I to tell God that an Orthodox kosher vegetarian with two adolescent boys is such a bad thing?

Stephen and I have now been married six years. And we have brought three children of our own into the world—Sarah, Elana, and Elijah. It hasn't been easy building a life together with so many significant differences between us. But whenever we experience tough times in our marriage and we wonder how we'll ever find a middle ground, we remind ourselves of our miraculous meeting—proof to us that we are truly beshert.

AZRIELA JAFFE
Lancaster, Pennsylvania

The Christmas Coat

PERSONALLY AND PROFESSIONALLY, 1991 was one of the worst years of my life. I had sunk into a depression that only got worse as the end of the year approached. The external and internal sources of the depression had spun my life out of whatever control I imagined I had. The holidays were always a difficult time for me anyway; the demands of the season with its hustle and bustle never seemed to be worth the effort, and somehow Christmas never lived up to my expectations. This attitude, combined with my circumstances that year, caused me to dread the season even more. I wanted only to hide out in my house. The necessity of shopping, visiting relatives, and attending holiday parties was torture for me and filled me with despair.

The Saturday before Christmas was a beautiful day. The sun was shining and the sky was blue. The air was crisp and clean, and the temperature was in the fifties. It was more like fall—my favorite season—than winter, but it did little to lift my spirits. I decided to take a walk, hoping the sun and fresh air would help dispel my gloominess. I went to our hall closet to get my light fall jacket. As I searched among the jumble of coats and jackets, I noticed a winter coat that I had picked up at a flea market several years earlier. The coat, while not expensive, was both practical and very large. I'm a big guy—six feet tall, two hundred and fifty pounds—and I could wear this coat over a sweater and sport coat and still have room left over. It was medium blue, all cotton, with a quilted lining. I had stuffed the coat in the closet after buying it, had never worn it, and had promptly forgotten all about it. But this day, as soon as I saw it, a small voice inside me said, "Wash it."

Strangely, I followed this thought and took the coat downstairs to our laundry room, where I ran it through the washing machine. Rather than use the dryer, I decided to take advantage of the nice weather and dry it outside on the line. I then went for my walk. Unfortunately, this did little to cheer me up. Just before sundown, I noticed the coat out on the line and went to bring it in. The coat had cleaned up nicely and smelled wonderful after having been dried outside in the crisp December air. As I returned it to the closet, I wondered what had prompted me to clean it, but then I soon forgot about it once again.

That evening, a bitter cold front moved in. The next morning, I built a crackling fire in our fireplace and my wife joined me to read the Sunday paper in our warm, cozy family room. In the local section of the paper I noticed a feature article about Sarah's House, a homeless shelter in our area.

The article described the staff, the people who lived there, and the limited services the shelter was able to provide. The story went on to explain that the shelter could accommodate only a limited number of men because of a shortage of beds and that the maximum length of stay for a man was thirty days. One of their current challenges was a man who would be forced to leave because of the thirty-day rule, turned onto the streets in the cold of winter with no winter coat.

In spite of my melancholy state, I felt immediate empathy for the man and a fair amount of guilt as I sat in my easy chair before a warm fire on this freezing Sunday. My eyes grew wider as I continued to read of the shelter's plea for anyone to call who might have an extra-large coat to donate before this man's departure. Feelings inside me began to stir as I remembered the coat that I had washed and dried the day before. I pondered the "coincidence." Suddenly that same undeniable voice inside said, "Call."

I dialed the number of the shelter and spoke to a pleasant woman who explained that unfortunately, the article had not clearly stated their need. As it turned out, their plea had brought in a slew of coat donations, but this man was huge, and a standard extra-large coat would not be sufficient. I assured her that I thought I might have exactly what she needed. I got dressed, grabbed the coat, and told my bewildered wife that I was headed for the shelter.

I found the building with no difficulty, parked, and walked into the reception area. I waited a moment while the staff appeared to be dealing with their latest crisis—a can of paint that had inadvertently been spilled by some active children. A woman finally noticed me and asked if she could help me.

I explained that I had just called about the coat. Then, without saying another word, I held it up in front of me. The women working in the reception area started cheering.

"Oh, how wonderful! At last! It's big enough, it'll fit!" I handed the coat over amid exchanges of "Merry Christmas! Thank you kindly!" I'll always remember the look of joy on their faces over a gift for someone else.

I have given and received thousands of gifts in my lifetime, but giving the gift of my coat that year brought a warmth to my soul I hadn't felt in a long time. For in that brief moment I was outside my personal misery, thinking of someone else. Perhaps it was the anonymity of the gift, or maybe it was because I expected nothing in return, but that simple act allowed me to feel good about myself because I had helped another. I didn't know it at the time, but this incident represented a turning point for me in how I would come to value the meaning of Christmas and my purpose in life. I pondered the "voice" that had led me to this place. Where had it come from? What was this all about? At the time I had no relationship with God; I believed I was responsible for my own destiny and thought that I alone controlled the events of my life.

Unfortunately, in 1992 things got worse. I became more isolated and desperate. At my lowest moment, however, that same "voice" returned and gave me the gift of guidance. Now I really began to listen to its counsel. No matter how bad things got, this guidance, which I finally accepted as coming from God, was always there for me. Over time I developed a relationship with God around which I rebuilt all the other relationships in my life. The joy of giving of myself became the key to my inner peace and happiness. As I reduced or eliminated my expectations of others and focused on helping them, I was transformed.

Christmas, too, has been transformed for me, becoming a time for sharing God's love with those around me. Gone are the fear, anxiety, and apprehension that used to cause me such despair. The day I gave the coat away I knew that to the extent we give to others, the world responds in kind. I never met the man who needed the coat. I hope someday, somehow, he will know of the miraculous gift he gave me.

GEORGE E. RALEY, JR.
Rising Sun, Maryland

A Life to Save

I'D WAITED FOR years for this moment: the moment when my twelve-year-old son and I set out on his first hunting trip, just like my father had taken me, and his father had taken him. We went out into the Pennsylvania woods to a special spot I knew of, far from the other hunters—to a remote hill that we would have to ourselves.

We put a lot of planning into the trip, and we decided to take my three young nephews along as well. A real "guy's weekend," with one big guy and some little guys out in the woods with guns. It was opening day of buck season, and we were ready. Daybreak was still several hours off when I backed the borrowed van out of the driveway. The four boys were wide-awake despite the early hour—too excited about the adventure ahead to go to sleep.

I am a very safety-conscious hunter and was well aware of

the kinds of things that could go wrong with five hunters and five guns. We would be hunting in a large gamelands area, each one of us in our own sector. I decided that I would hunt the middle area so that I could hear all of them from my position. We made a base camp so that we'd have an area where we could all meet throughout the day to eat and get warm. I built a fire, and we agreed that we would all meet up in a few hours for lunch.

The boys started off right away, eager to get out into the woods. As planned, I hunted down the middle of the hill, always aware of the movements of the boys. After a few hours of hunting had passed with no sign of a buck in my sector, I returned to the camp to begin fixing sandwiches. As I busied myself with the task, I thought about how pleased I was with the way the day had turned out. This day would give my son and his cousins a childhood memory that they could always treasure. And I, too, would look back on this day and smile. I hadn't yet spotted a buck, but perhaps one of the boys would. Pleasant thoughts ran through my mind as I sat in front of the campfire assembling bread, bologna, and cheese. This would be a good day in the woods.

A good day, yes, but suddenly I was feeling tired. Tired from working a double shift as a prison guard the night before, tired from packing all the camp gear, tired from getting up early enough to drive out to this remote spot. I thought about the energy of those four young boys and knew I'd need to catch my breath if I were going to keep up with them. Maybe I could just lie down and close my eyes for a moment . . .

I was jarred awake as the van hit a bump in the rutted dirt road. Where were we? Why was I lying on the floor in the back of the van? I should be driving—these kids aren't old enough to drive. Why did everything seem so fuzzy and my mind so confused? Was I dreaming?

"How is he?" I heard my nephew Eddie shout.

"I'm not sure," my son Paul replied, his voice noticeably shaken. "He keeps waking up and then going back to sleep. Can't you drive any faster?"

But of course Eddie couldn't drive any faster, because he didn't really know how to drive. At fifteen, he'd had only limited experience behind the controls of a car, and none at all with a stick shift. But there he was, trying desperately to drive a five-speed van carrying a heavy load on a remote dirt road. The load? Me, his uncle, badly burned and only semi-conscious.

It was Eddie who'd found me lying there in the fire. He'd gone back to the camp to check on lunch and found me burning, in shock, and unable to roll out of the fire. Somehow, while I lay in a deep sleep, the fire had spread and caught onto a piece of my clothing. The doctors said later that as soon as the fire started burning me, I probably immediately went into shock and fell unconscious.

Dragging my deadweight away from the flames as best he could, Eddie shouted to attract the attention of the boys still out hunting. Together they had managed to half drag, half carry me through the woods to where the van was parked—a two-hour mission in itself and a feat made more miraculous considering the swampy, rough terrain and rock walls they had to lift me over. Now I was in the van and headed for the hospital, but at a snail's pace of just a few miles an hour down an old logging road, with a frightened fifteen-year-old boy behind the wheel.

Slowly, in my groggy state, it dawned on me that I was in trouble. Real trouble and real pain. It was hard to maintain consciousness, but I tried as hard as I could. Eddie needed my help driving the van. Through excruciating pain I had to try to give him detailed instructions about how to work the clutch. Every time we came to a hill the van would stall and get stuck.

"Let the clutch pedal out as slowly as you can, Eddie, while you gently press on the gas pedal at the same time." But sometimes, through a fog of pain, my comments were less detailed. "Mary will help you do it. Mary will guide you," I assured him when the van became stuck yet again.

"Mary?" Eddie asked. "Mary who?" I smiled later when I learned how baffled my Mormon nephew had been by the assurances that I, his Catholic uncle, had offered him.

At last we reached the highway, but the journey wasn't over. Eddie still had to drive the van to the hospital. Where was the hospital? We were in unfamiliar territory. Rather than wasting time trying to find a nearby hospital, Eddie chose instead to drive all the way to a hospital that he knew: the one in his town—fifty miles away. Another long, frightening journey for a teenage driver.

The doctors swarmed over me in the emergency room. "We've got full thickness here—second-, third-, and fourth-degree burns over forty-five percent of his body. We need all the help we can get," the first doctor on the scene cried. I was barely aware of what was happening by that time, but relieved to know that I was in a hospital at last. I could hear the doctors as they worked on me, talking about what they found, what they were doing. But then there was something else they were discussing.

"And the baby? Could you save the baby?" I heard one ask another.

"The ambulance staff revived him, and then lost him. We tried twice with no luck. I think it's over."

A baby? Was there a baby who needed the doctors' help in this same hospital? I'm not sure how clearly I was thinking at that point, but I distinctly remember thinking that the doctors should turn their attention back to that baby. They shouldn't waste time on an old guy like me, I thought; they need to try to save the little baby. A baby had so much more ahead of him, so much more to do in life . . . I needed to tell them that. If they have to choose whose life to save, they should choose the baby.

"Save the baby," I whispered gruffly to the doctors leaning over me. "Please go and save the baby, not me. Don't worry about me . . . please go!" They exchanged glances over my gurney, and after I continued pleading, they quickly left the room to try to revive the baby one more time. Somehow, on their fourth attempt, they were able to revive the baby boy, and he lived. He was an unfortunate little guy who had nearly been suffocated when his neck had become stuck in his toy chest.

What I didn't know at the time was that as my nephew, Eddie, had rushed into the hospital that afternoon, he was startled to see his sister, Chris, standing there. "I'm so glad you're here!" he said, assuming that she had somehow learned that their uncle was in serious condition.

"And I'm so glad that you're here!" Chris replied, thinking that her brother had rushed to the hospital upon hearing the news that her two-year-old son, Joshua, had been rushed to the hospital in an ambulance. It was little Joshua who had been discovered unconscious, his neck trapped in a toy box.

Somehow, in my semiconscious state, I knew that my doctors couldn't give up on that tiny life in the next cubicle. Something inside me kept urging me to insist that they try to save him. But it wasn't until many days later, while still recovering in the hospital, that I found out that the child whose life I had urged the doctors to save was in fact the youngest member of my own family. What if I hadn't insisted that they try one more time to save the baby? What if I hadn't even been at the hospital that day? Would there have been a heartbreaking funeral to attend that very week? I shudder every time I think about it and thank God that I listened to the voice inside.

And so I had to wait another year to take my son Paul out for the opening of buck season—a year of painful recovery from my burns. But the day arrived at last when we were once again together in the beauty of the Pennsylvania woods: a thirteen-year-old boy, happy to be walking through the golden fall leaves with his healthy—and very grateful—father.

JOHN PITCAVAGE
Swoyersville, Pennsylvania

A Perfect Pot of Tea

AN IMPATIENT CROWD of nearly two hundred die-hard bargain hunters shoved their way into the huge living room of the old Withers home. The sweltering ninety-degree temperature didn't deter a single one of them, all in hot pursuit of the estate-sale find of the summer.

The woman conducting the sale, a longtime acquaintance, nodded knowingly as we watched the early-morning scavengers snatch the remainders of a privileged lifestyle. "How's this for bedlam?" she asked, chuckling.

I smiled in agreement. "I shouldn't even be here. I have to be at the airport in less than an hour. But when I was a teenager," I admitted, "I sold cosmetics door-to-door in this neighborhood. And Hillary Withers was my very favorite customer."

"Then run and check out the attic," she suggested. "There are old cosmetics up there that you wouldn't believe."

Quickly, I squeezed through the throng and climbed the stairs to the third floor. The attic was deserted except for a petite elderly woman presiding over several library tables loaded with yellowed bags of all shapes and sizes.

"What brings you all the way up here?" she asked as she popped the stopper out of a perfume bottle. "There's nothing up here besides old Avon, Tupperware, and Fuller Brush products. All the fancy things are downstairs."

I drew a long, cautious breath. The unmistakable fragrance of Here's My Heart perfume transported me back nearly twenty years in time.

"Why, this is my own handwriting," I exclaimed as my eyes fell upon an invoice stapled to one of the bags. The untouched sack held over a hundred dollars' worth of creams and colognes . . . my very first sale to Mrs. Withers. The years suddenly fell away as I recalled the wild excitement I'd felt the day I realized that some people were really rich enough to purchase more than a hundred dollars' worth of cosmetics at one time.

On that long-ago June day, I'd canvassed the wide, tree-lined avenue for nearly four hours, but not one lady of the house had invited me indoors. Instead, several had slammed their door in my face. As I rang the bell at the last house, I braced myself for the now-familiar rejection.

"Hello, ma'am. I'm your new Avon representative," I stammered when the carved oak door swung open. "I have some great products I'd like to show you." I fixed my eyes on the hem of the homemade skirt I'd proudly stitched in sewing class. I'd tried so desperately to dress and act like the fashionable saleswomen at our district meetings. Yet despite all the rehearsing at home in front of our bathroom mirror, my efforts had been woefully inadequate.

When I finally found the courage to look at the lady in the doorway, I realized it was Mrs. Withers, the bubbly soprano in our church choir. I'd often admired her lovely dresses and hats, dreaming that someday I'd wear stylish clothes, too. Just two months earlier, when I'd traveled to a distant city to have brain surgery, Mrs. Withers had showered me with the most beautiful cards. Once she'd even tucked in a Scripture verse: "I can do all things through Christ which strengtheneth me" (Philippians 4:13). I'd carried it to school in my red vinyl wallet. Whenever my teachers told me I'd never make it to college, I'd take it out and study it. I'd believed that verse, even when my teachers kept saying, "With all the school you've missed, Roberta, you can never catch up." I don't think they meant to be cruel. Perhaps they felt it was kinder not to let me dream too much, since I was afflicted with neurofibromatosis, a serious neurological disorder.

"Why, Roberta, dear, come in, come in." Mrs. Withers's voice sang out with delight. "I need a million and one things. I'm so glad you came to see me."

Gingerly I eased myself onto the spotless white sofa and unzipped my tweed satchel, chock-full of all the cosmetic samples five dollars could buy. When I handed Mrs. Withers a sales brochure, her twinkling eyes caressed me. Suddenly I felt like the most important girl in the whole world.

"Mrs. Withers, we have two types of creams, one for ruddy skin tones and another for sallow skin," I explained with newfound confidence. "And they're great for wrinkles, too."

"Oh good, good," she chanted warmly.

"Which one would you like to try?" I asked as I adjusted the wig hiding my stubbly, surgery-scarred scalp.

"Oh, I'll surely need one of each," she answered. "And what do you have in the way of fragrances?"

"Here, try this one, Mrs. Withers. They recommend that you place it on the pulse point for the best effect," I instructed, pointing to her diamond-and-gold-clad wrist.

"Why, Roberta, you're so very knowledgeable about all of this. You must have studied for days. What a fine, intelligent young woman you are."

"You really think so, Mrs. Withers?"

"Oh, I know so. And just what do you plan to do with all of your cosmetic earnings?"

"I'm saving for college—uh—I'm going to be a registered nurse," I replied, surprised at my own words. "But today I'm thinking more of buying my mother a cardigan sweater for her birthday. She always goes with me for my medical treatments, and when we travel on the train, a special sweater would be so nice for her."

"Wonderful, Roberta, and so considerate, too. Now, what do you have in the gifts line?" she asked, requesting two of each of the items I recommended.

When I tabulated her extravagant order, I was stunned to find it totaled $117.42. Had she meant to order so much? I wondered. Would she now cancel part of it? But she only smiled at me and said, "I'll look forward to receiving my delivery, Roberta. Did you say next Tuesday?"

I was preparing to leave when Mrs. Withers said, "You

look absolutely famished. I bet you've been walking all afternoon. Would you like some tea before you go? At our house,
we think of tea as 'Liquid Sunshine.' "

I nodded enthusiastically, then followed Mrs. Withers to
her pristine kitchen, filled with all manner of curious oddi-
ties. I watched, spellbound, as she orchestrated a full-scale tea
party of the kind I'd seen in the movies—just for me. She
carefully filled the teakettle with cold water, brought it to a
"true" boil, then let the tea leaves steep for "exactly" five long
minutes. "So the flavor will blossom," she explained. Then
she arranged a glistening silver tray with a delicate china tea
set, a charming chintz tea cozy, tempting strawberry scones,
and other small splendors. At home we sometimes drank iced
tea in jelly glasses, but never had I been a princess reveling in
the genteel ritual of afternoon tea.

"Excuse me for asking, Mrs. Withers, but isn't there a
faster way to fix tea?" I asked. "At home we use tea bags."

Mrs. Withers wrapped her arm around my shoulders.
"There are some things in life that shouldn't be hurried," she
confided. "I've learned that brewing a proper pot of tea is a
lot like living a life that pleases God. It takes a little extra
effort, but it's always worth it. Take you, for instance, with
all of your health problems. Why, you're steeped in determi-
nation and ambition, just like a perfect pot of tea. Many in
your shoes would give up, but not you. And with God's help,
you can accomplish anything you set your mind to,
Roberta."

Abruptly, my journey back in time ended when the lady in
the hot, sticky attic asked, "You knew Hillary Withers, too?"

I wiped a stream of perspiration from my forehead. "Yes. I

once sold her some of these cosmetics. But I can't understand why she never used them herself or gave them away."

"She did give a lot of them away," the lady replied matter-of-factly. "But somehow, some of them got missed and ended up here."

"But why did she buy them and then not use them herself?" I asked.

"Oh, she purchased a special brand of cosmetics for her own use." The lady spoke in a confidential whisper. "Hillary had a soft spot in her heart for door-to-door salespeople. She never turned any of them away. She knew they had so many doors slammed in their faces. She used to tell me, 'I could just give them money, but money alone doesn't buy self-respect. So I give them a little of my money by buying their products, a listening ear, and my love and prayers. You can never be sure how far a little encouragement can take someone.' "

I remembered how my cosmetic sales had really taken off after I'd first visited Mrs. Withers. I'd bought my mother the new sweater from my commission on her sales, and still had enough money left over to feed that all-important college fund. I'd even gone on to win several district and national cosmetics sales awards. Eventually I'd put myself through college with my own earnings and realized my dream of becoming a registered nurse. Later I'd earned a master's degree and a Ph.D.

"Mrs. Withers prayed for all of these people?" I asked, pointing to the dozens of timeworn delivery bags on the table. I felt the lump in my throat grow bigger.

"Oh yes," she assured me. "And she did it all without even the slightest desire that anyone would ever know. That was

Hillary. She looked for a quiet way to serve, then left the rest up to the Lord. For Hillary, it was a secret investment as sure as any bank account."

At the checkout table I paid the cashier for my purchases—the sack of cosmetics I'd sold to Mrs. Withers and a tiny heart-shaped gold locket. Later, in my car, I threaded the locket onto the gold chain I wore around my neck. Then I headed for the airport; later that afternoon I would address a medical convention in New York.

When I arrived in the elegant hotel ballroom, I found my way to the speaker's podium and scanned the sea of faces— health-care specialists from all over the country. Suddenly I felt as insecure as on that long-ago day peddling cosmetics in that strange, affluent neighborhood.

Can I do it? I questioned myself.

Then my trembling fingers reached upward to the locket on the long chain around my neck. It swung open, revealing the picture of Mrs. Withers inside. Her eyes seemed to look directly into mine, and over the long span of years I again heard her soft but emphatic words: "With God's help, you can accomplish anything you set your mind to, Roberta."

"Good afternoon," I began slowly, "thank you for inviting me to speak to you about 'Putting the "Care" Back in Health Care.' It's an oft-repeated and totally accurate cliché in my profession that 'Nursing is love made visible.' But just this morning I learned an unexpected lesson about the power of quiet love expressed in secret. The kind of love expressed not for show, but for the heartfelt good it can do in the lives of others. Some of our most important acts of love, I've discovered, go seemingly unnoticed—that is, until they've had time to steep, time for their flavor to blossom."

Then I told them my life-changing story of Hillary Withers. To my surprise, there was thunderous applause. Silently I prayed, Thank you, God—and thank you, Mrs. Withers. And to think that it all began with a perfect pot of tea all those many years ago.

The hotel staff wheeled in steaming teapots and trays of sumptuous croissants. The convention moderator glanced at her watch. "Looks like it's time for our afternoon tea break," she announced with a grin.

Yes, indeed, I thought, anticipating the moments of fellowship that lay ahead. Perhaps a pot of tea would work a few more wonders of love.

ROBERTA L. MESSNER, R.N., PH.D.
Huntington, West Virginia

Papa!

IN THE EIGHT months I have lived in Mexico, I've learned a lot about judging people's true character. In the small town of Anáhuac where my wife and I run an orphanage, most of the people are very poor, and you have to look past their worn clothes and simple houses to see the richness of their souls. Mostly, I have learned to look at their eyes.

Becky and I had come to do some work at this orphanage several times over the last few years through the sponsorship of our church. After realizing how much help the people needed and after seeing how desperately poor they were, we decided to make our contribution more permanent and committed to a five-year stay. We had two wonderful grown daughters and I had been blessed with much success in my career, so we felt it was time to give back a portion of the many blessings we had received in life. We had no idea that our experience in Mexico would prove to be much more of a renewal of our souls than a sacrifice.

The orphanage is called Casa de la Esperanza, which means House of Hope. For the fifty or so children who live here, it is exactly that. These children have nothing; many have been abandoned by their parents and have lived in unimaginable conditions for many years. But even with their poverty and their past, most of them have a light in their eyes that speaks of faith and hope for a brighter future.

It was at Christmastime here that I really recognized that light among so many. I've enjoyed many wonderful holidays over the years in the luxury and comfort of home in the United States. Surrounded by family and friends, I have celebrated the season with all the normal festivity and tradition—the lights, the music, the shopping, the parties, the tinsel and ornaments—that most American families take for granted. And I have enjoyed the gifts of the season—the new clothes, electronic gadgets, luxuries, and toys—given lovingly on those special occasions. But never before have I felt the depth of love that I felt in the midst of these humble children—who had nothing to give—on my first Christmas at the orphanage.

The night of our celebration, all the children were dressed in what to them was their Sunday best. They had prepared special decorations and had helped set the table carefully. As a special treat we had turkey for dinner that night, and a savory aroma filled the air. After we ate, everyone joined in singing Christmas carols. There was a small tree in one corner of the room and underneath it, a simple shoebox for each child. The moment they all waited for, when each of their names would be called and they would come up and receive their shoebox, had finally arrived.

The first child to be called was Oscar, a small and shy five-year-old, who jumped to his feet at the sound of his name. With both hands in his pockets and a sheepish look of antic-ipation on his face, he slowly crossed the large floor to receive his gift. The group became silent as everyone's attention focused on him. Suddenly, when he had gone halfway across the room, there was the sound of clapping. As if paying trib-ute to a king, one little girl started clapping for Oscar as he approached his Christmas shoebox. One by one, others joined in until the whole room was applauding for him. And so it went for each child whose name was called—clapping and more clapping. The children simply couldn't contain their happiness for each other.

In the days following our Christmas party I noticed some-thing different about the way these children played with their gifts compared with what I had observed among American children. Although each child had received just a small box of candies and little plastic toys, they were happy to share whatever they had with each other. I never heard complaints of "that's mine" or "give it back." In fact, after the initial excitement of opening the boxes, no one even seemed to be aware of what belonged to whom. The joy of simply having received a gift spilled over and created a very generous atti-tude among the children.

But, in fact, it was shortly before Christmas that I really became aware of the good hearts of these people. It was then that I met the seventy-six-year-old man, José Enriquez, or

P a p a !

"Papa." I had received a call from someone at the Mexican Department of Social Services (or DIF, as they call it) asking whether we could take in a little Indian girl who had been found in the streets near the town square. No one knew her name, her age, or where she was from, because they couldn't understand the Indian dialect she spoke. We agreed to take her. Upon arriving at the DIF offices to pick her up, I saw a little girl sitting in a chair, legs and arms crossed, clutching a tiny rag doll in her hands. It was obvious that she had been living in the streets for many days. Her face was dirty, her dress was soiled and faded, and she wore only one sock. And on her face—in her wide brown eyes—was an expression of horror.

Behind her frightened stare, though, was a beautiful child. With stone-black hair, almond eyes, and dimpled, round cheeks, she was truly one of God's lovely creations. When we attempted to take her back to the orphanage, she cried hysterically; obviously, her recent experience had taught her to trust no one. She had been found by police officials wandering in the town plaza, hungry and somewhat dazed. We learned later that her mother was dead and she had never known her father.

By the end of the first day with us she settled down a bit, finally trusting that no one was going to hurt her. We made up a bed for her, and by nighttime, she had relaxed and was playing with some of the other children, although she still appeared to be on guard and somewhat bewildered. Because the Indian people in this area live in such squalor, our humble Casa must have seemed like a palace to her, and she took in all the surroundings at the orphanage with a sense of awe.

Two days passed and little Angelica (which we had learned was her name) was beginning to warm up to us. On the third day, around five o'clock in the afternoon, we had a visitor. An old, weary man walked up to the orphanage. Too thin from lack of food and appearing as if he had been wearing the same clothes for weeks, his dark, lined face and leathery hands told of a hard lifetime of working in the sun. He was hunched over and wore an old straw cowboy hat. I thought he was just another villager looking for work—yard work, perhaps—and I would have to tell him that all the positions at the Casa had been filled. But as he approached, something drew me to him.

It was his eyes. They were kind and loving and there was just a spark of hope left in them, though I could tell his life had given him every reason to be cold and bitter. His dialect was unfamiliar to me, but his eyes told me he had come to the orphanage seeking something far more important than a job. He held out a worn piece of paper, trying to explain something to me that I couldn't understand. When he insisted that I look at the piece of paper, I realized it was a picture of someone, although it was obviously a third- or fourth-generation photocopy and the image was difficult to make out.

Then I saw it. The hope in his eyes and the pleading in his voice were suddenly clear to me. The picture was of Angelica. She was his beloved five-year-old granddaughter. He had been searching for three weeks, posting these flyers with her picture in every town between here and his home of Chihuahua, ninety miles away.

My heart skipped a beat as I thought about the miracle of his finding her. What if he had come here earlier in his search, before Angelica's arrival, and we had sent him on his way? Angelica had been with us only two days, but she had been missing for three weeks! What if Papa had given up what seemed like a fruitless search in a country that contains millions of poverty-stricken children?

Over the next few hours Papa shared with us his story. He had walked for fifteen days through the crowded streets of his city of half a million people, returning home each night, worried and heartbroken. He later explained that he couldn't even bring himself to turn on the lights at home each night because he would see his granddaughter's belongings throughout the house. He continued on to Cuauhternoc, a city of 150,000 people, and, after several days of searching there, walked twelve more miles to Anahuac. Now, after twenty-one weary days of searching, he had ended up at the orphanage.

With the last of his money spent on making photocopies of the flyer, the old Tarahumara Indian man hadn't eaten in days, and had slept only when he could, along the streets of each city. I would later learn that this kind man had taken in a hungry teenager some months before, but returned from work one evening to find both the teenager and Angelica gone. Many young children in Mexico are sold through a black market, and this was probably the teenager's intent with Angelica, but somehow this little girl had managed to escape.

After it dawned on me that the girl in the picture was

really Angelica, I looked up at him and smiled. I slowly nodded my head yes and saw his discouraged expression change and his eyes light up with surprise and joy. We walked down the hall together, and I left him there with my wife while I went to find Angelica. He must not have heard her coming, but when he turned around and saw his little granddaughter, he slowly reached up with one hand to remove his hat while the other hand covered his eyes to hide his tears. He struggled to kneel so he could embrace her as everyone stood and watched the joyous reunion. "Papa! Papa!" Angelica cried as she ran the short distance into his arms. They didn't speak, but just held each other and sobbed. And so did we.

As José and Angelica ate dinner with us that night, I looked down to see them holding hands under the table. They hardly took their eyes off each other, needing reassurance that they had indeed been reunited and that their frightening journey had finally ended.

They would return to their village the next day, but I knew in my heart that the image of this man and his angelic granddaughter would be with me forever. As I pictured José walking day after day, week after week, through the dry dusty streets of each city, I realized I was sitting next to a man who understood the meaning of devotion in its purest sense. As I thought of him trudging along without food in his stomach, money in his pocket, or a change of clothes on his back, with hope as his only guide, I no longer worried about the care Angelica would receive during the rest of her childhood. Her papa had not let her down, and I knew he would love her as no one else could as as long as he lived. After all, I had seen it in his eyes.

GIL SANCHEZ
Anáhuac, Mexico

If you would like more information about Casa de la Esperanza, please contact Gil Sanchez: children@infosel.net. mx.

The Gift of Silence

I N THE EIGHT years since the time I was baptized with my grandmother in the wading pool behind the choir pews at church, I had fallen out of the habit of attending church very often. My life was just too hectic and there were more important things for a young man to think about. Once in a while during those years, though, I would get this feeling—a strange pull at my stomach or tug at my heart—almost like God was trying to tell me something, trying to get me to do something for Him. But I never stopped to listen.

When I woke up that sultry summer day in 1996, I knew something was wrong. I was listless and my body ached all over. With a slight sore throat, I thought I just had a common cold that would be gone in a few days. Sure enough, the cold finally went away, but when it did, so did my voice.

It was August when I started having trouble speaking. It's not that I didn't have the ability to speak, but whenever I attempted to use my vocal cords, the pain was excruciating. It felt like my throat was on fire with razor blades. I simply didn't know what the problem was and I was afraid to find out. After two weeks of this, however, I went to see my doctor and then a specialist. Neither could come up with a diagnosis. It was very frightening, to say the least.

At the time I was a substitute teacher of high school history and the school year was just beginning. Have you ever seen a teacher who couldn't speak? Well, the district administrators hadn't either, so they let me go—until my voice healed, they said.

I began to use paper and pen for communication in my new silenced life; they were my constant traveling companions. If I went to a movie, I would write down the name of the film I wanted to see and give it to the attendant at the ticket counter. If I went to a fast-food drive-through, I wrote down my order and handed it to the person at the window. I used paper and pen to communicate with my family for the most part also. The only exception was my five-year-old daughter, Mackenzi, who couldn't read my writing yet. So I whispered to her. I would put my mouth as close as I could to her ear. It amazed me how quickly she adapted to our new form of communication.

I went from specialist to specialist—about a dozen in all—but none of them could say why my voice had disappeared or when it would return. Some of them recommended exploratory surgery, but that idea frightened me even more than the situation I was in, and I kept putting off the decision. After five or six weeks my attitude started to change. I found I was psychologically preparing myself to live the rest of my life as a mute. Since even whispering caused extreme pain, for all intents and purposes I was mute. I was no longer scared, nor was I bitter. But I learned to accept my situation without blame or self-pity.

In October, after two months of not speaking, I decided to teach myself sign language. After all, I needed to be prepared for the long haul. So I borrowed books from the library and spent several hours each day learning the basic skills in order to communicate in sign language.

My world had come to a standstill, and in that stillness I was silent. And it was there in my silence that God spoke to me. I suddenly felt that I had an important work to do. I felt He was calling me to the ministry—to be a preacher. It was that same tug-at-the-stomach-or-heart feeling I had experienced at times during the years I hadn't been going to church and had felt on occasion that God was trying to speak to me. Only this time it seemed to make even less sense. How could someone be a preacher without a voice? But now I had nowhere to run, no options, no hectic life to escape to that could help cover up the feelings.

So on a Sunday morning in January, after not speaking for almost five months, I returned, a stranger, to the same church in which I had been baptized years before. I didn't recognize anyone there and no one knew me. I walked up to Reverend Lyn O'Berry, pad in hand, with a note scrawled on it. It read: "My name is Bobby. I'm a mute and I would like to discuss the possibility of entering the ministry." The reverend and I met and "talked" for three hours the next day about life, God, and my belief that I had been called to preach.

Reverend O'Berry didn't have all the answers for me, but he knew the power of God. He suggested that I start attending church regularly and see what the Lord would provide. But then, when he learned that I had been studying sign language, a light of understanding filled his eyes. He told me that ever since Thanksgiving the members of his congregation had been searching for someone who knew sign language. They were anxious to find someone who would provide the service for free so they could begin an outreach ministry to the deaf community, who had nowhere nearby to go for services. And shortly afterward, although I didn't know it at the time, this good congregation started praying for me.

Within a couple of weeks after the prayers began, my voice completely returned and I was able to speak normally again. My silence was broken. It was an incredible feeling to be able to talk to my friends and family again. Mostly, I wanted to tell everyone how grateful I was to God and His power to perform miracles. Some people may have thought that I was healed as a consequence of all the gargling and throat lozenges I was using, but I knew differently.

Our church now has a ministry to the deaf and I continue to teach sign language to other church members. We'll always need more people with this skill because we don't want the deaf to have to be segregated when they come to church. We want them to be a part of the congregation's family.

I am now convinced that God uses a variety of methods to

get our attention when He needs it. He gave me the gift of silence to help still my soul and make me quiet enough to hear His loving voice.

BOBBY GAWTHROP
Brooklyn, Maryland

The Miracle on Sherbrooke Street

ONTREAL USED TO be known as the "City of Churches." The role of the church in the city has declined somewhat over the years, but the influence can still be seen in the way that all of Montreal embraces the Christmas season. The efforts of residents, merchants, and city workers alike turn the city's wide boulevards into a glittering fantasyland ablaze with decorations and lights. And it was on one of those wide boulevards that our Christmas miracle occurred.

I was the president of the community council for Notre Dame de Grâce that year. One of my duties involved organizing a big public caroling party. We wanted to involve not just church members, but as many people from the surrounding community as we could. Christmas is a wonderful time of year to reach out, and we hoped that our party, "A Christmas Caroling," would accomplish that. We invited many choir members (and anyone else who could carry a tune) and friends to join us one night on the sidewalk of Sherbrooke Street.

Sherbrooke Street is a wide downtown street lined with stately old elm trees. The heavy branches of the trees were gaily decorated with colored Christmas lights, which were reflected in turn on the dark, slick streets below. It was a magical look. The turnout was great, a group of thirty-five adults and children all bundled up against the snowy night, clutching songbooks in their gloved hands. A multitude of voices soon filled the air as we warmed up with a few of the old Yuletide favorites—"Hark the Herald Angels Sing" and "The Twelve Days of Christmas." I was excited; this community event was everything I'd hoped for, with one small exception. It was *cold*.

Our plan was to stand on the sidewalk and sing for passersby instead of going door-to-door. As we assembled to begin, I noticed a few singers look longingly into the frosted windows of a restaurant behind us. The restaurant was pleased at the presence of such a large group of singers and had even offered to give us all free hot chocolate that evening. I decided that the time for hot chocolate had arrived.

The group of singers filed one by one down the eight narrow stairs that led into the small restaurant, grateful that a warm drink was on its way. We stood together in the center of the room, waiting for our group to reassemble at the tables. A small parade came slowly down the stairs. It took a few minutes before the last of our group stepped into the restaurant. And then it happened.

No sooner did we all sit down than a loud crash rang out.

The underground building shook, and we rushed up the stairs toward the door. And there, at the very spot on the sidewalk where our large group of singers had stood just moments before, lay a large electrical truck, its broken wheels spinning. The driver of the Hydro-Quebec truck had lost control on a patch of black ice as he drove down Sherbrooke Street and had crashed head-on into the street lamp.

We did sing our carols that night. Too shaken to stand out on the street again, we stayed down in the restaurant and sang for the truck driver, the police, and the owners of the restaurant, whose generous offer of hot chocolate had spared us all.

STEPHEN LAUDI
Montreal, Canada

Links to Love

Y FATHER OWES a debt of gratitude to a man he never met.

I read recently that 90 percent of all Father's Day gifts eventually wind up in cold storage in a dresser drawer or closet. Every year, when discussions turn to the day that honors fathers, I think of my own dad's private stash of presents, now relegated to his bureau drawer. To a casual observer, the whimsical assortment of four-inch-wide polyester ties, purple socks with DAD stitched on them, and a finger-painted picture framed with Popsicle sticks, would appear hopelessly impractical and outdated. But among the dime-store and homemade mementos that have long outlived their usefulness is a Father's Day gift that changed my family forever. It was purchased twelve years ago, all because of the prompting of a stranger, and to this day it's a token of my family's love and quiet strength.

On that warm June day many years ago, my patient lying on the clinic examining table—with his silver hair, red plaid shirt, high-bibbed overalls, and smell of Old Spice—bore a striking resemblance to my dad. He was an all too vivid reminder of the painful secret Dad had confided the evening before. "I'm a hopeless alcoholic," Dad had wailed over the phone, his speech slurred. "I've got to stop drinking. If I go on like this, it's going to kill me. You're the nurse in the family. You help all those other people. Why can't you help your drunk old dad?"

My dad a hopeless alcoholic? I thought that term was reserved for skid-row bums, not for wonderful, kind people like Dad. Being an alcoholic just didn't fit the image I had of Daddy, who'd once walked a mile in the snow at midnight searching for my tattered teddy bear. Could the generous neighbor who'd mobilized our entire block when the Esteps' home burned down actually be an alcoholic? The father who'd held down two jobs to provide for our family?

When I really thought about it, I'd suspected Dad was drinking more heavily since his retirement from the railroad three months before. But Mother, embarrassed that someone at church might find out, downplayed it all—his growing hostility and criticism over the least little thing . . . the fact that he rarely left the house anymore except to go to the liquor store to fuel his fifth-of-whiskey-a-day habit.

"I've tried to talk to your dad about his drinking," Mother confessed one day. "But he just stares off into space and I feel so sorry for him. The other evening, he told me, 'They say a chain's only as strong as its weakest link. Well, I guess I'm the weakest link in this family.' "

When I was in high school, Dad began to drink heavily on weekends. Although it never appeared to affect his job, the liquor did aggravate his stomach ulcer. "I can take or leave the stuff," he'd claimed. Amazingly, he had managed to stop drinking—until retirement, when he suddenly had too much time on his hands. In a matter of weeks alcohol began to mean everything to him.

My patient's soft, Southern voice interrupted my reverie. "How's my liver, Nurse?" he asked.

I methodically pressed my fingertips over his entire abdomen. "Everything seems to be normal," I answered. "You say you've been getting along all right? No more pain or bleeding?"

"Yeah, I'm doing fine. This coming Saturday I will have been sober for four solid years. No more alcohol for me."

"You have a drinking problem?" I gulped, thumbing through his thick medical record. "How did you ever manage to stop?" I prayed that he would tell me how to help Dad, all the while hoping that he wouldn't see through my professional facade. "Do you have a family? Did they help you?" I asked.

My patient peered at me over his black bifocals as he got off the examining table, his eyes as turquoise as a perfect June sky. "I still have to constantly be on guard," he admitted, "but the main thing is to face the fact that you have a problem and get the help you need. That help has to come from within yourself, from the people all around you, and from Someone greater than all of them."

Then, as he turned to leave, he looked me square in the eye. "Nurse," he said, " there is something else." He hesitated for a moment, and his eyes took on a faraway look of fatherly wisdom. "When I was in my treatment program, there was a man there, another alcoholic. Joe was his name. His kids gave him one of those medical-alert bracelets and engraved 'We love you' on it. Deep down I wished that could have been my bracelet. I always wondered what it would be like to know for sure your family loved you."

Three days later Dad took his last drink, vowing never to drink again. Going without alcohol made him so ill, however, that Mother couldn't manage him alone. The three of us children stayed with him in shifts and watched helplessly as the withdrawal wreaked havoc on his body. When Dad thought he'd spotted spiders on the kitchen wall, he finally agreed to check into the hospital.

After visiting him one evening, my brother and sister and I stopped in the hospital cafeteria for coffee. Our discussion turned to the upcoming Father's Day and what we might buy Dad. "You pick it out, Jane," Ann insisted. "You always think of good presents." I stared into my coffee as my patient's haunting words played over and over in my mind. Eventually I mustered the courage to suggest the bracelet.

"You can't be serious," Tom retorted. "Dad hates jewelry. Says it's always in the way. Why, he never even wore that fancy locomotive watch we gave him last Christmas. It was a limited edition and it's buried under a bunch of junk in that drawer of his. Besides, he doesn't go in for that sentimental stuff."

I remembered Dad's words when we'd handed him that watch. "Now, you kids don't need to be spending your hard-earned money on me. Every day is Christmas with a family like you." It was the closest he'd ever come to saying "I love you."

Then Ann piped up. "I know it's a slim chance, but I think the bracelet idea is worth a try. Dad is on that special medicine. Maybe he'd wear it if he thought it was medically necessary."

The next morning, the three of us found ourselves downtown at the jewelry store staring into the big glass showcase. We selected a silver, chain-link medical-alert bracelet with our message inscribed on its underside: "We love you, Dad. Tom, Jane, and Ann."

On Father's Day, as we drove to the hospital, we prayed that Dad would somehow know we cared about him and that God would give him the strength to stop drinking once and for all. "Now, you won't have to wear this forever," we explained as he tore open the gift wrapping. "Just while you're on your medication."

Three weeks later Dad was discharged from the hospital. Every hour he struggled to learn to live without alcohol. One day he called us all together. "Something happened to me while I was in treatment, there with all those guys who'd lost just about everything because of booze," he said. "One afternoon my doctor said to me, 'If you keep on drinking like this, you'll be dead in a year. Now, you've told me a lot of reasons why you drink—your parents died when you were just fourteen . . . you feel guilty for working so much when your kids were growing up . . . you're down on yourself now that you've retired. But if you're going to tackle this drinking problem, you've got to find a reason not to drink.'"

Dad looked down at the sturdy silver bracelet and smiled.

"I was nervous when the doctor said that, and plenty scared. I felt like no one in the world could love me for all the trouble I'd been. Then I started twisting that confounded bracelet and found those words: 'We love you.' There was something permanent about them. They were something no one could take away from me. I had a reason—a good reason—not to drink."

Dad never again touched a drop of alcohol. The links in that glistening bracelet became a symbol of the many steps our family would take in learning how to cope with his recovery from alcoholism.

Recently, as I was leaving work for the day, I felt a tug on the sleeve of my lab coat. A silver-haired patient with turquoise eyes and a soft Southern voice whispered, "Nurse, is your dad still on the wagon?"

"How did you ever remember me after all this time?" I gasped. "And how did you know it was my dad I was worried about that day in the clinic?"

"Oh," he answered, "I could never forget you. It was your eyes. Those pleading eyes. They were just like my Judy's the day she begged me to stop drinking. Over and over she begged. But I wouldn't do it. I just couldn't do it. I lost my family because of alcohol."

"It's been twelve years since Dad took his last drink," I said. "And that bracelet you told me about was the perfect gift. It was his new beginning—a new beginning for our whole family. Until then, we'd never actually said the words 'I love you.' "

Later that day I rummaged through Dad's bureau drawer until I retrieved his old medical-alert bracelet, still untarnished. I caressed its strong links and in my heart I thanked God that with Him there are no weak links that cannot be made strong again.

It seems to me that Father's Day gifts have gotten some bad press lately. So many of those tangible expressions of love, though often tucked away in a dresser drawer or closet, never really outlive their usefulness.

JANE BLEVINS
Tupelo, Mississippi

Radio Days

M Y CHILDHOOD WAS *filled with stories, stories that boasted colorful characters, lively dialogue, and wonderful settings. Best of all, each story taught a valuable lesson. Children's books, you say? No. Although I did my share of reading the beautifully illustrated fairy tales and nursery rhymes, the stories that filled my childhood were not written down. They were spoken.*

Night after night as I lay in bed with the hand-stitched quilt drawn up under my chin, I listened in the dark as my mother, my father, a grandparent, a visiting uncle, or older cousin would fill the nighttime silence with stories of life in the old country—Italy. Or even tell stories of life in the new country—America.

I loved these family stories. Each one gave me a clearer picture of my ancestors, or a better understanding of the relatives I already knew. One of my favorite nighttime stories was of my great-

*grandpa and his radio, and how it helped him learn the real mean-
ing of friendship.*

Papa Vincenci nestled comfortably into his rocker and,
with a twist of his hand clicked on the dial of his brand-new
RCA Victor radio. It was Papa's habit each night, after one of
Mama Savadia's robust Italian meals, to position himself by
his beloved radio and tune in the nightly antics of radio characters: Fibber Magee and Molly, Amos and Andy, Edgar
Bergen and Charlie McCarthy, and the Lone Ranger.

There were no complexities to Papa Vincenci's lifestyle;
his wants and needs were easily satisfied by a good meal, a
warm home, and a loving family. He lived his life by the simple and old-fashioned creed "Pray for the things you want,
work for the things you need."

If Papa had one luxury, it was the household radio he had
acquired. The radio had become a vital component in his
daily life. It restored his energy and brought back his sense of
humor after a long day working as a tree pruner in the fruit
orchards of the Santa Clara Valley. With the impending
arrival of World War II, the economy had begun to tighten,
but the budget-wise Grandpa had managed to scrimp and
save enough money from his meager earnings to purchase the
new radio. Although Papa had known poverty in the old
country, he felt he'd never been poor, only broke. Being poor,
Papa believed, was a state of mind; being broke was only a
temporary situation.

Papa loved his new radio, but Great-Grandma preferred
listening to her old Victrola or puttering around her woodstove to sitting by the radio. Until the day she heard her first
episode of *One Man's Family* on NBC radio. This show was

about a strong, loving family, something Great-Grandma could relate to. From that moment on, she was an ardent fan of the new medium.

In time Great-Grandma came to believe the radio had been sent to them as a blessing. It had helped both her and Papa Vincenci to learn better English, and it had been a boost to their social life as well. The radio gave them a common topic to discuss with their neighbors, who listened nightly to the same radio programs.

On warm summer nights, Papa sat on his front stoop with his neighborhood cronies, Mr. Goldstein, Mr. Miller, and Mr. Rosenberg, discussing their favorite radio programs. There were times when Mr. Goldstein would explain the meaning of a certain Yiddish word Papa had heard on the Molly Goldberg show. Other times Papa would translate a Puccini opera for Mr. Goldstein. Some nights the old friends had a good laugh at the expense of the contestants on Ted Mack's *Amateur Hour*. The radio had helped to bond these old friends, who came from vastly different backgrounds, in a way few things could. These men had left their old country to escape tyranny and oppression, and as young immigrants they settled into the neighborhood together. Although they came from varied parts of the world and followed different religious beliefs, they shared a love for their new country and family traditions.

And so their friendship grew until that fateful December day in 1941 when Papa's radio brought him the terrible news that Pearl Harbor had been attacked. He would hear President Roosevelt declare war with Japan and with the Axis powers, Germany and Italy. It was a declaration that would change Papa's life.

The knock on Papa's door came early on a December morning in 1941. It brought with it a special-delivery letter from the government of the United States declaring that Papa must surrender all radios on his premises—*effective immediately*! All people of Italian heritage who lived near the East or West Coast were subject to this ruling. The American government was worried that shortwave radios would be made out of home radios and that vital secrets might be passed to the enemy.

Papa Vincenci had no political ties to his former country. He had worked and lived in America for over thirty years and had raised his children and grandchildren as honest, hardworking American citizens. But the fact remained that he was a native of Italy, a country now ruled by the fascist tyrant Benito Mussolini, who had chosen to side with the Axis powers against the United States.

As Papa read the dispatch, tears of indignation rolled down his face. Losing his radio would be sad enough, but Papa was more concerned that he might lose the company and respect of his friends in the community, which he had earned during the thirty years. More than anything else, Papa prided himself on his honesty and high moral standards. His word had always been his bond. Now he feared that a war thousands of miles away had cast a shadow over him.

It appeared Papa's fears were well-founded: Some of his employers, leery of Italian immigrants, had begun canceling their job offers. Papa worried that his longtime friendship with the Goldsteins, the Rosenbergs, and the Millers was also in jeopardy. Would they also view him differently now? Could they somehow believe that he shared the same political beliefs as the terrible tyrant Mussolini?

That Christmas Eve, Papa and Great-Grandma sat quietly in their favorite chairs warming themselves by the fire. Papa couldn't help but miss the raucous sound of his radio, and the daily banter with his friends and neighbors, which he feared he had now lost as well.

A knock on the door brought Papa to his feet. Opening the door, Papa was surprised to find his old pals the Goldsteins, the Rosenbergs, and the Millers standing on his front stoop.

Mr. Goldstein was the first to speak up. "Vincenci, my friend. The United States government says that you can no longer own a radio, is this correct?"

Wearing a quizzical expression, Papa answered, "Yes . . . yes, this is so."

"But the government did not forbid you should listen to a radio, correct?" inquired Mr. Rosenberg.

"Correct," Papa answered.

Papa's neighbors handed him a sheet of paper. On the paper was a handwritten schedule listing the broadcast time of all of his favorite radio programs. Each entry corresponded with a neighbor's address. His old pals had gotten together and worked out a radio listening schedule for Papa and Great-Grandma that included every show from Molly Goldberg to *Little Orphan Annie*.

"Read it, my friend. It's all there," said Mr. Rosenberg. "You and the missus will listen to *Fibber McGee and Molly* at the Millers' house. Tuesday: Ted Mack's *Amateur Hour* and *The Goldbergs* at my house. Wednesday: *Edgar Bergen and Charlie McCarthy* at the Goldsteins'. Thursday: *The Lone Ranger* and *Jack Armstrong* at the Smiths' house, and so on, until all of your favorite programs are accounted for. You won't miss one of your favorite shows if we can help it, Vincenci."

Papa's eyes welled with tears, but this time they were tears of joy and gratitude. Papa invited his dear friends into his house to celebrate. While Great-Grandma served freshly baked biscotti, Papa filled each glass with homemade red wine.

Before going to sleep that night, Papa and Great-Grandma said a silent prayer of thanks. Papa had lost his valuable radio on that somber day in 1941, but what he'd found in friendship on that Christmas Eve was truly priceless.

COOKIE CURCI-WRIGHT
San Jose, California

The Usher

Y WIFE AND I aren't bad people, but we did make fun of the usher. Everybody did. He had a name tag pinned right over the front pocket of his ludicrous fake tuxedo jacket, but neither of us ever looked at the name on it as we entered the theater for our weekly Saturday matinee. To us, he was just "the usher."

The usher was in his thirties. Overweight. Big glasses. Cheap plastic tennis shoes from the dollar store, fitting companions to his tight, polyester dress slacks. My mom had a saying about people like him: not the smartest brick in the schoolhouse. It was another way of saying what he really was. Slow. Challenged. Mentally handicapped.

He had a nervous tic that sometimes came out when too many people arrived at once and backed up at his ticket box. His chubby hand would fly to his forehead. One finger would point out crookedly and he would tap himself while small, quiet squeaks slipped from his mouth.

Most of the time, however, especially on those slow Saturdays, there weren't many people in the place. The usher really took center stage at those times. He would take our tickets, one at a time, and rip them in half with a grandiose flair before handing them back promptly. Then he would give my wife directions. "Ladies first," he always said politely. "You will find your movie down the hall. Take your first left, go twelve steps, take another right, then go left. Thank you. Come again." He spoke to each person as if they were royalty. Then, before he let me through, he would repeat the same directions, word for word, as if he hadn't seen us hugging and exchanging bites of fresh popcorn and sips of cold soda on the way to his shredded-ticket box!

We would always smile when we were past him, and one time the manager caught us doing so.

"Isn't he amazing?" the middle-aged man in his burgundy jacket remarked to us good-naturedly. "He gets here an hour early every day just to make sure his directions are correct. I tell him the movies are in the same spot every day, but he's afraid there might be a mix-up one day and so he comes in early to check on them just the same. Says he hasn't gotten the directions wrong yet."

One Saturday it was crowded. Thanksgiving was coming and the push was on for those special-effects blockbusters and weepy, big-star dramas that rack up huge ticket sales over the holidays. The usher reeled off his precise, detailed directions for customer after customer. Several ticket holders complained that he was taking too long, and the usher began to sweat, squeak, and tap his forehead with his crooked finger.

Someone hushed the complainer with a not-so-quiet "Leave the poor kid alone. Can't you see something's wrong with him?" The usher paused only a moment before continuing with his directions, but my wife and I both knew the comment had been made loudly enough for him to hear. I wondered if a guy like that had the mental capacity to get his feelings hurt. When it was our turn, we listened patiently to his directions and thanked him profusely. On our way into the theater we scolded each other for ever making fun of the usher in the first place.

The theater was packed and we sat up front. The previews went on forever and the noise was deafening. We felt bulky in our coats, which were filled with stray popcorn kernels.

I noticed the smell of smoke even as my wife began sniffing. My eyes started to sting just a little and the movie grew blurrier by the second.

Mumbling began and seats squeaked as people turned to each other to ask if they smelled the smoke, too. The movie continued, yet the mumbling grew so loud that it was impossible to hear. Suddenly the double doors burst open and a flashlight beam cut the thick smoke in half.

"Please proceed to the nearest exit," said a stern voice above the mumbling and sound effects. "Walk away from my voice and don't panic. Move row by row, and toward the movie screen. Exits are to the left and the right of the movie screen. I repeat . . . " The voice was familiar; the emergency procedure script had been well memorized.

Even though we were up front, the crush of bodies in the crowded aisle prevented us from leaving our seats at all. The smoke was thick now, and the movie was still running, mixed with the sounds of shouts and yells. People cursed and shoved more forcefully as the smoke grew thicker, yet above it all that calm, firm voice insisted that people move forward, toward the screen.

"To the left and right are exits," he kept saying. "Move toward the movie screen . . . "

Finally, with tears streaming from our eyes from the thick smoke billowing through the movie theater, my wife and I made it to the aisles. I gripped her arms firmly as we were swept toward one of the open exit doors by the crowd behind us. Outside the theater, patrons gathered in grumbling clumps as my wife and I bent over and sucked in deep breaths of fresh, cold air.

We waited while the rest of the theater emptied. The crush of guests thinned out slowly until they were emerging one by one. Finally, a little old lady was helped out by a chubby man in a fake tuxedo.

But the usher took no time for praise. He made sure the woman in his care was all right, and then disappeared back into the theater. Despite our cries and shouts to the contrary, he ran straight into the smoke.

There were more theaters to empty. More directions to give. More lives to save.

Cellular phones beeped in nearly every hand and the 911 switchboard must have been overloaded. Soon fire trucks came and hoses blasted the main lobby of the neighborhood theater, where an oil-encrusted popcorn machine had caught fire.

The theater manager in the burgundy coat berated the teenage movie workers who had gathered out front to goof off and smoke as soon as the movie started. Had they been manning their posts, none of this would have happened. Tears filled his eyes as he continued to search the crowds in vain for the usher who had directed the people with such efficiency.

"He wasn't even supposed to work today," the manager cried to no one in particular as he searched the crowd for the chubby, caring face of his favorite usher. "But he knew we'd be busy and came in anyway."

The crowd grew silent as an ambulance screeched through the chaos, sirens blaring, leading the way for the two massive fire trucks that followed. Helmets and axes, hoses and spray soon filled the air as rescuers battled the smoke and firemen blasted the blaze.

We waited anxiously for word of survivors. Gasps and applause rippled through the crowd like the wave at a football game as two burly EMT drivers hustled a last group of stragglers through the crowd and straight to the ambulance doors.

Several people wiped tears from their eyes as a somber ambulance crew emerged from the smoky theater with a heavy stretcher covered in a soot-stained white sheet. They had found the usher. My wife and I clung to each other, the manager's words echoing in our ears: "He wasn't even supposed to work today . . . "

But it seemed there was a reason for him to be at work that

day. A divine, heavenly reason that assured the safety and survival of all those living, breathing moviegoers left in his heroic wake. The usher may have been gone, but his example of concern for others at all costs—the miracle of his dying act—would live on in all of our hearts for a long, long time.

JOHN RICHARD
Greensboro, North Carolina

Blessings from Saint Peter

ONE OF THE earliest Christmases I can remember was in the seaport town of Perth Amboy, New Jersey, where I was born. The deadly epidemic of influenza swept our poverty-stricken nation, touching every neighborhood with sickness or death. We were in the midst of the Great Depression and there was little or no work. Many were starving; others were begging in the streets or traveled illegally as hobos on freight trains, in search of employment. Most parents could not find work for years. A few of my older siblings found meager, part-time manual labor for pennies an hour in the larger city of Newark or in nearby New York.

I was the youngest boy, one of nine children. My parents emigrated to America from Eastern Europe. We lived in a humble home across the street from four rows of busy railroad tracks. Smoky trains, the lifeline to New York City, rumbled past our house regularly. My sisters and their neighborhood girlfriends would sometimes stand by the railroad tracks waving at the hobos. They undertook this dangerous pastime with the slim hope that the hobos might be able to help them. And sometimes they did. The hobos would occasionally throw down the precious fuel, coal, to the girls. Sometimes, from fruit trains, itinerants would toss apples, oranges, grapefruits, and bananas in the same dangerous manner. Many times our sisters came home with their aprons full of treasures; other times, nothing—the trains were empty.

My young ears often heard the words "depression, foreclosure, poverty, repossession." But our parents' devout religious faith kept us all appreciative of what we had and helped motivate us toward righteous desires. It was always "God's will"!

My crying siblings and pleading parents begged the grim stranger who appeared one day not to repossess our family radio, but he did anyway. Yet from this sad moment I was inspired to go to the library for a book on how to build radios. With this knowledge and with parts from the trash cans of a radio shop, I built a small crystal radio that worked to entertain our family until better times. Who would have dreamed that this gloomy moment for my family would set my feet on the path of a successful career in electronics?

Mother always had a way of jumping in at the right time with her words of wisdom—or sometimes threats. "Children, stop crying about the radio, or I'll find something for you to do. There are a lot of chores to be done. Christmas is coming."

Our older brother Charlie said, "I'm going to tell my neighborhood buddies who watched us get repossessed that my mother made them take back the radio, because we were having too much fun listening to it and not doing chores."

Mom said, "No lying, wise guy! Come here, I have a special job for you." Mom then told Charlie, "On Christmas Eve, you take your brother Stevie, since he's the tallest, and you both go down to the Christmas-tree lot and get us a beautiful tree."

Charlie laughed. "And what should I use for money? It doesn't grow on trees, you know!"

"Don't be funny," Mother said. "You know I scrub floors and clean house once a week for that rich family across town. The lady of the house gave me an extra dollar for Christmas and their old dog for you kids. But the main thing is, her brother-in-law owns a Christmas-tree lot down the street. Moe always gives away all the unsold trees at eight P.M. on Christmas Eve. Be there, up front. Bring home a big, beautiful tree, and make it a fresh one. It has to last until our Christmas on January seventh, the real Christmas day."

We always celebrated two Christmases and got off from school for both. There was the American one on December 25 and the Ukrainian one on January 7. We didn't get more presents, but we sure went to church a lot.

"But, Mom," Charlie protested, "we tried that last year! Mr. Moe threw the unsold trees into a crowd of about thirty men and boys, and if you caught one you still had to fight to keep it. Moe would only have about twenty bad-looking left-over trees anyway!"

"If it's God's will, you will try harder this year and bring home a tree; after all, you are a year older and stronger. No more talk, get busy."

Dad got part-time work with the city, working outside all day in the bitter cold, repairing streets. He was paid one dollar and given some old World War I surplus food. He happily came home with several cans of meat, cheese, prunes, and small bags of potatoes and flour. My mother's genius would have to provide food for the multitude of our family, plus visitors, for our two Christmases.

On Christmas Eve, after eight o'clock, Charlie and Stevie proudly arrived home with a large, beautiful tree. They looked like they had had a tough fight to keep it, but they were victorious. My proud mother clapped her hands with delight and thanked God and my brothers. Dad and we boys immediately started to decorate it. Our large cherry-red stove in the kitchen not only provided the heat for our home, but also baked and cooked the great feast my mother planned to perfection. The night rang with the sound of carols sung in several languages.

Dad gave out our Christmas presents; we had a choice of either an apple or an orange. I was the last and had to settle for an apple, for that was all that was left. We sat down to the banquet my parents had provided, which looked and smelled delicious. My father stood up and said grace, then passed around holy bread, honey, and a taste of the sacramental wine. Dad continued with the blessings, thanking God for the beautiful Christmas celebration, and for good health, wealth, and happiness.

How my mother heard a soft knock on the door through the joyful caroling I will never know, but she did. Mom opened the front door, letting in the cold wind and some blowing snow. Several strangers waved at her from the street as they entered their car. "Merry Christmas!" they shouted, and drove away through the dark and snowy night. Mom returned the salutation and was closing the door when she noticed a large colorful object on the dark porch. She asked my two older brothers to help bring it indoors.

We all came over to see the mysterious, colorfully wrapped basket of food now sitting on the living room floor. Through glistening transparent paper the basket revealed a large, dressed turkey, fruit, vegetables, bread, cans of nuts, candy, and soft drinks, all wrapped with a bright red ribbon.

Our parents were speechless. We children all looked at the basket and at each other. We each had our eye on what we wanted from the basket, but no one touched it, because we were not sure it belonged to us. My older sister Ann sheepishly moved through our ring of spectators and said to my perplexed parents, "Mom, Dad, I know about this Christmas gift basket; it was given to us by the people of St. Peter's Church from across town. They are not of our faith, but they give out these baskets to the poor and needy."

Our youngest sister asked, "Are we poor and needy?"

I said defensively, "We are like everyone else in this neighborhood. Why did they leave it here?"

My sister Sal said, "I didn't know we were poor, Ma. Everyone knows the Schultzes on the next corner are very poor. They have ten children and their father is desperately ill." While we debated our poverty level, our parents had their own private discussion.

Mom told everyone to go back to the dinner table, for Dad had something to say. "Family and friends, we thank St. Peter's Church for this generous and bountiful gift. Yes, today we are financially poor, but so is everyone else we know. Yes, we are poor, but we are not needy. We have a good church, and God will provide for our needs. We are healthy, but one of our neighbors is not. We are very blessed and we know how to share, and we will. Amen! Please, everyone, enjoy the feast around you."

While we returned to our Christmas Eve dinner, our parents excused themselves, put on their heavy winter clothes, picked up the large Christmas basket, and went out into the snowy night. They returned home shortly after leaving the basket by the front door of our destitute neighbor.

After dinner we dressed for a late-evening church service. There was a loud knock on the door. Cold neighborhood Christmas carolers entered, singing joyfully. Our family joined in and we invited our visitors to stay for hot cider and cake. The jolly entertainers told us that one of the most jubilant homes they had visited earlier was down our street. A very poor family had miraculously received a beautiful Christmas basket and was overjoyed. "Merry Christmas!" we shouted and smiled as we all left for church.

EDWARD ANDRUSKO
Boulder, Colorado

The Bracelet Promise

HE GLITTER OF green stones drew me to the display case. The light bounced off silver and glass. Amid the throng of holiday shoppers, I stood in the corner area reserved for fine jewelry and gazed at the bracelet, noticing its unique handiwork. The beaten silver, fashioned to resemble diamond chips, was exquisite, and it was encrusted with dozens of dark green emeralds. I knew this was a one-of-a-kind treasure.

As I admired the intricate piece, I remembered a promise my husband had made. David had bought me a lovely gift on our honeymoon four years earlier. He had selected an emerald-green Austrian crystal and seed-pearl bracelet in honor of my May birthstone. As he fastened it on my wrist, he lovingly said, "I promise you that I will buy you real emeralds someday soon. Just wait." I loved the sentiment of his honeymoon gift, but deep down I excitedly looked forward to the fulfillment of David's promise.

Until that time, however, I still loved wearing my crystal bracelet. I wore it frequently, each time fondly remembering the island boutique where we had found it. Whenever David saw the bracelet, he would smile and reassure me that the time was coming soon when he would keep his promise.

It became our habit over the years to look in every jewelry-store window, as if searching for the Holy Grail. David's pursuit became symbolic of his devotion to me, and I loved him for it. We wandered in and out of countless shops, becoming somewhat discouraged when we realized that the cost of his promise was well beyond our means. I started to doubt that I would ever own what David desired to give me. David, however, never lost faith.

On the day I found the particular bracelet, we were in the mall during the last week before Christmas to buy gifts for our children. Finances were tight and we had agreed there would be no exchange of gifts between us. We had just completed one of the most stressful years of our marriage. With David's diagnosis of Huntington's disease, our lives had forever changed. This fatal neurological disorder had pitched us into a panic, not to mention near bankruptcy.

I looked up into David's eyes and saw love shining even brighter than the green stones. I could tell what was in his mind: Nothing short of this bracelet would satisfy his original honeymoon promise. But I knew there was no way we could possibly afford it. I tried to tell him, but the words died on my lips. He'd had so many disappointments that year; I didn't have the heart to tell him that we absolutely shouldn't consider it.

Thinking fast, I came up with a reason to refuse the offer I knew I couldn't accept. I have large wrists and normally bracelets don't fit. As the store clerk reverently lifted the object out of the case, I knew it would be too small. The silver and green made a colorful contrast against my brown skin. I silently acknowledged how much I wanted the bracelet while still hoping it would not fit. As the clerk reached around my wrist and closed the intricate clasp, my heart both leaped and then quickly plummeted. It fit! It was perfect. Yet I knew it would be wrong to buy it. The unpaid bills, with more looming in the future, had placed a vise around our checkbook.

I glanced at my husband, my best friend, and saw him beam. This gentle man was now the victim of a very cruel disease. His was a sentence with only one verdict: untimely, slow, and cruel death. My eyes brimmed with tears as I realized we would not live out our dream of growing old together. The jewelry before me was meaningless compared with the hope of living a lifetime with this man. But to David, the bracelet on my wrist would not be just one more bauble in a crowded jewelry box. Rather, this was his love for me displayed for all the world to see. To David, a promise made was a promise to be kept. I sadly realized that he might not have many more months or years in which to keep his promise. Suddenly it became the most important covenant ever made, and I knew that somehow I had to juggle the bills to let him have the honor of keeping it.

"Do you like it?" he whispered. Hearing the hope in his voice, mingled with the adoration in his eyes, was heart-wrenching. It was clear that David cherished me. All he ever wanted, from the day we met, was to make me happy. I was a lucky woman, indeed.

I heard myself saying, "Yes, honey, I love it. It's exactly what I want."

The clerk reached out to remove the bracelet. I could not believe this little object had worked its way into my heart so quickly. "How much is it?" I finally asked. Slowly the man turned over the little white tag. Two hundred and fifty dollars. Surely this was a mistake! I had seen enough fine jewelry to know that that price was only a fraction of its worth.

The man began to extol the beauty of the item, pointing out the one hundred eighty emeralds in a handmade Brazilian setting. But even though $250 was an incredible value, it might as well have been $2,500, given our meager budget. Without thinking, I asked, "Would you take two hundred twenty-five dollars, tax included?" I was amazed to hear myself ask the question, because shops in malls do not normally bargain. The clerk looked at me in surprise but answered, "That will be fine."

Before he could change his mind, I whipped out my credit card, watching David beam with pride. The man quickly handled the transaction and we were on our way. Every few steps we would stop and look at the bracelet. Before we reached the car, David said, "When I get sicker and eventually am no longer with you, I hope you'll look at each emerald on the bracelet. Every one will remind you of something special we've done: a trip we took, a movie we saw together, or a moment we shared. This will be your memory bracelet."

I began to cry. David's concern was not for his own failing health, but for my welfare after he was gone.

As we worked our way home in rush-hour Honolulu traffic, I wondered just how we would pay for the bracelet. Oddly enough, however, I never really panicked. I was somehow only curious about how it would all work out. We talked as we drove, and every so often we looked admiringly at the miracle of the promise kept.

Upon arriving home, I grabbed the mail and began to open it as we walked inside. Among the usual bills were two cards. One was from a church where I had sung several times that year. It was a thank-you note for my music ministry, along with a gift. It was a check for two hundred dollars! I was speechless! I reached for the second card and slit it open. Out fell two bills: a twenty and a five. The card was simply signed "A friend in Christ."

I looked up at David and we both shook our heads in amazement and then began to laugh. Even as I had inexplicably felt the urge to negotiate our price in the mall, the payment for David's promise was in our mailbox. God had already taken care of every detail, right down to the penny. The promise David made on our honeymoon had been fulfilled. It was only because of God that we stopped at the shop to find that specific bracelet. The pastor of a small church, together with an unknown friend, listened to God as they decided upon their holiday giving.

The bracelet is just a piece of jewelry, something I could

have lived without. But the memories represented by each emerald have helped make me the person I am today. The exquisite joy of our relationship and the unspeakable grief of dealing with David's disease have allowed me to develop in ways I never could have anticipated. I have thought about God's promise to each of us—that He will be with us every step of the way in life, if we will just ask Him. Just as God has never stopped believing in me, David never stopped believing in his bracelet promise. Each time I wear my emeralds, I count the memories tucked away in my heart, and I feel new courage as I think about David's faith and God's promises.

CARMEN LEAL-POCK
Lake Mary, Florida

Visions of Michael

HEN MY WIFE and I went to bed on the evening of August 19, 1986, we were both excited about our baby's impending birth. I had attended childbirth classes so I could participate, and we both felt prepared. The entire process intrigued me. I knew what to expect during labor and transition, and I felt confident that I could really help Susan throughout the delivery. We knew that the baby was a boy and his room had already been decorated with blue wallpaper. With Susan's bags packed and our journey to Pennsylvania Hospital in Philadelphia well rehearsed, we were ready and eager for the big event.

Our baby was to be named Michael, like me, and we were going to call him Mick. I believe that every child who comes into the world is a special gift from God, and Mick would certainly be no exception. Each night during the last months of Susan's pregnancy, I'd rub her back and legs. I almost felt reverence for this body that was carrying our precious gift. Then I would try to talk to Michael through Susan's firm belly. I would say, "Hello, Michael! This is Daddy. Over." I'd wait to see if Michael would answer back—which he often did with a kick in my ear.

On this particular night in August we knew that Susan's time was drawing near, and as we tried to doze off, we both kept wondering if we'd be waking up in just a few hours to rush off to the hospital. Finally, I found myself in that very deep state of rest, when all of a sudden my spirit seemed to be fully conscious and wide-awake. I felt very much aware that someone was calling my name.

"Michael," I heard.

My first thought was that the voice was God's and I remember the feeling of "Oh, no!"—fearing that I was being "called home." I heard my name called a second time and then I saw an image of little Michael inside Susan's womb. The vision was dark and had a reddish glow, as if someone had turned on an extremely bright light positioned on the other side of Susan's stomach. I could see Michael moving and then I heard a voice clearly say, "The umbilical cord is wrapped around his neck twice." The voice, which I knew came from the Lord, repeated these exact words again to me and I was able to see the baby from a slightly different angle. This time I could actually see the cord wrapped around his neck.

Then the image was gone. I felt fully awake, as though my spirit had just reentered my body. Instead of being frightened, I felt strangely calm and in control—somehow encouraged that I could handle the challenge I felt certain lay ahead of us. Lying there next to Susan, I tried to think things through logically and decided that the best thing to do was to roll over and get some sleep. I knew that I'd need my energy the next day.

In the morning Susan woke up with all the symptoms indicating she was in labor. I was absolutely certain that I would have a job to perform as well that day, but I wasn't sure exactly what it would be. With last night's experience rooted deep in my heart, I felt surprisingly at peace. But with all the excitement and nervousness of getting ready to go to the hospital, I thought it was best not to mention it to anyone at that point. After making all the appropriate calls, we collected our bags and started our thirty-five-mile trip into Philadelphia.

By the time we reached the hospital it was early evening. Everything was going according to plan. Susan's labor seemed to be right on track, and after she was settled in a bed and hooked up to monitors, I sat by her side and tried to be as supportive as possible while her labor continued. I could see the baby's heartbeat on the monitor, but as I watched it carefully, I started to see the same image from the night before. The feelings that accompanied this vision were a strange mix of urgency—knowing that I should reach out and do something about it—and that same familiar sense of calm I had had the night before. But after an hour or two I suddenly realized that the little guy was fighting for life on his own and I was the only one aware of it. That's when I ran to get the delivery-room nurse.

Trying not to sound like a fanatic, I told the nurse outside Susan's room about my experience. I carefully explained how the Lord had told me about the umbilical cord and I tried to convince her that if they let the labor progress any further, the baby would go into fetal distress. The nurse went right into the room and checked the monitor output and then reassured me that everything looked normal.

Knowing that I couldn't give up, I tried another tactic. Using all the logic I could muster, I said, "You know, sometimes in life it's not good enough to say you have faith—faith also requires action. And there are times when you have to act! What would you do if God had given you such a vision—would you ignore it?"

She studied my face for a long moment and then said, "Okay, let me see if I can get you some suction." Of course, I had no idea what she was talking about, but I breathed an enormous sigh of relief. At least she was going to take some kind of action, and I had a feeling that faith was about to move a mountain!

The nurse went to get Susan's doctor, who had been sleeping until things progressed further. After checking the monitor, he came out and, just as the nurse had done, assured me that everything was going very well.

"I know you think everything is going well, but you don't know about the dream I had last night, warning me about the baby's condition," I urged. He looked at me skeptically and turned to the nurse as if to say, "Is this guy crazy or what?" The nurse looked him squarely in the eye and responded only, "Suction, Doctor?" I started to think that I was going to be vacuumed up or something, but when the doctor said, "Okay," I again felt relieved that something was going to be done. When the nurse exclaimed, "Praise God!" I thought I would faint.

It was now the early-morning hours of August 21, and the medical staff started preparing Susan to go into the delivery room. I still had no idea what "suction" meant, but I reminded the doctor again that the cord was wrapped around Michael's neck twice. The doctor didn't acknowledge what I was trying to tell him but turned his attention instead to a second doctor entering the delivery room.

I was expecting a long medical procedure of some kind, but suddenly an instrument was produced that resembled a toilet plunger with a stainless-steel handle. The word "suction" was beginning to take on meaning! Before I had time to think about what might be happening, the instrument was placed inside Susan, who, thankfully, was sedated. Just when I thought we were getting started, Susan's stomach wrenched and the bulge moved down and out of her body in one powerful movement. Michael was born instantly.

Both doctors seemed a little anxious as one remarked to the other, "The cord was wrapped around twice." Unable to keep quiet, I said, "I just need to double-check that you meant the umbilical cord," to which the doctor nodded yes vigorously as his eyes nervously danced up and down above his surgical mask. Michael was whisked away to be checked, but Susan needed some more attention. The umbilical cord had broken, so the placenta had to be removed by hand.

Considering the circumstances, Michael was in great shape when I went in to see him. The delivery-room nurse told me there was no damage to his neck and that he was a very fortunate little fellow. Our kind nurse jokingly asked me if I now knew what "suction" meant and we both laughed out loud. I ventured to ask her what she thought about my vision and she answered tenderly, "Michael is a miracle baby." The doctor might have been shocked, but she was not. She hadn't found it very hard to believe that the father of an unborn child might be given a special heavenly message if it could save the baby's life.

Now a healthy, active boy of twelve, Mick continues to bless our lives. Because I know it's my responsibility to love and nourish this gift from God, each year of his life I try to become a better caretaker. I've come to rely more and more on faith in my role as a father, and—as I learned firsthand from Michael more than twelve years ago—sometimes faith requires action. I try to remember to use a little of both.

MICHAEL STEIN
Philadelphia, Pennsylvania

The Quiet Man

I WAS FACING Christmas alone for the third time. It had now been three years since my beloved husband passed away. He and I loved the holidays, and I had tried hard on my own to continue our traditions. I put up a real tree, built the little village underneath it, and put the tiny train together. I baked all of the family specialties and invited the children over for Christmas dinner— but it wasn't the same. It never will be.

We raised a large family together—three girls and five boys. And those eight children have now given me fifteen grandchildren. So it is a large crowd that gathers at my house every year for the holidays, and they all miss their "Papa's" presence just as much as I do.

That year, as usual, I attended the midnight mass at our parish church. The mass was, in fact, dedicated to my late husband, a bittersweet tribute and one that made me feel his absence all the more. Sitting in the smooth wooden pew, I let the music of the carols and the words of the sermon wash over me as my thoughts roamed back over my years with my husband, Dan.

We always called him the Quiet Man, a man more given to gestures than words. And his gestures over the years had been memorable—a bouquet of flowers for no particular reason; small gifts that would quietly appear at my breakfast table. My favorite surprise was the evening he came up behind me and slipped a small diamond necklace around my neck. "Just a little something to make up for the bad times," he said as he fastened it in place. Oh, he could make me smile, that husband of mine.

Even after his death, it sometimes seemed that he was still with me. The first Christmas without him was the hardest— at least it was until he made me smile. How did he do it? As I drove home from church that day, consumed by my new loss, I decided that a little Christmas music might distract me. I punched the button on the radio and settled back, expecting to hear "Silent Night" or "Angels We Have Heard on High," the typical Christmas Day fare. What came softly over the airwaves was Andy Williams's rendition of "Danny Boy," a strange selection for Christmas Day. It was a cheer-up gesture from Dan, I'm certain of it. And it made me smile.

Sensing my sadness after the special midnight mass ended, one of my grandsons offered to come home and spend the night with me. I thanked him, but decided instead to spend Christmas Eve alone with my thoughts. I went home to my gaily decorated—but empty—house and settled in comfortably by a cozy fire. One by one I read the lovely holiday cards and messages that I'd received. Instead of the sadness I'd felt on earlier Christmases, I had a feeling of peace. Before turning in that night, I quietly thanked God for all forty-six years that Dan and I had together.

Christmas morning dawned, and I set about preparing the house for the arrival of my family. My first task was to clean out the fireplace and lay a fresh fire. This had always been Dan's favorite job; he took particular care to build a long-lasting fire, with the logs and the kindling placed just so. I tried to take the same care, scraping out the burned chunk of wood from my fire the night before and sweeping out the ashes before setting the wood and kindling inside. I would wait to light it until the children and grandchildren began to arrive.

My daughter Ginny was the first to appear. She cooked up a sumptuous breakfast of scrambled eggs, bacon, toast, rolls, and freshly ground coffee. I put our holiday ham in the oven and sat down to the share this early-morning feast with her.

As we began to eat, Ginny said, "Gee, Ma, that's a great fire you built."

"Fire?" I asked. "What fire? I haven't started it yet. It is for later this afternoon."

"Well, turn around and look," Ginny urged. And turn around I did. There was the most beautiful fire blazing away in my fireplace, a fire that I hadn't struck a match to. It was one of Dan's fires.

My daughter and I sat together in the kitchen, marveling at the scene before us. Once again, it seemed that the Quiet Man was watching out for us, showing us with one of his small gestures that he was nearby and thinking of us. The warmth of the fire that year helped to melt away more of the sadness that my family still felt about the loss of their father. For now we knew that as lonely as we were without him, he was trying to let us know that we were still in his heart.

MARGARET H. SCANLON
Hamburg, New York

The Flight of Our Lives

Y THE TIME Thanksgiving rolled around in 1993, I wasn't sure whether I had anything to be thankful for. With a grown daughter who had been in and out of the emergency room all year, my heartache, my tears and fears didn't leave much room for counting my blessings. Nancy, our only daughter, had had diabetes since the age of three, and now, more than thirty years later, her kidneys were finally giving out. She had been on the kidney and pancreas transplant list for five months. If organs did not become available, her doctors had scheduled December 23 as the day she would need to start the painful process of dialysis.

On the morning of December 23, I got out of bed in a state of deep despair. It was a cold, gray day in Pikeville, Kentucky, with snow in the forecast. I didn't think I could face the thought of Nancy going on dialysis, knowing that it might be months or even years before a donor would become available with a matching blood and tissue type.

I couldn't believe it when my phone rang at ten A.M. that day and Nancy excitedly announced that her transplant coordinator had just called to say a donor had become available for her. Nancy was to be at the University of Cincinnati hospital in no more than five hours. Live organs are good for only a limited amount of time, and it was absolutely imperative that Nancy's surgery take place before seven P.M. that night. We had one major problem: we were three hundred miles away from the hospital!

Within an hour we were on the road to Cincinnati. Under ordinary driving conditions, it's a three- to four-hour trip, but the heavens had something else in store for us that day. Very shortly, the snow started falling and the highway quickly became slick and hazardous. It became increasingly clear that it would take us at least five or six hours to reach the hospital where the transplant was to be done. All we could do was keep hoping and keep driving.

As we drove, my husband, a ham-radio operator, kept talking to other hams on his two-meter rig, inquiring about the road conditions ahead. All reports were bad: The roads were quickly becoming covered with ice and traffic was becoming slow and heavy. Many cars were pulling off the road to wait out the storm, but we didn't have that choice. The clock was ticking for our daughter and our only option was to proceed as carefully as we could, praying that we would make it safely . . . and in time.

By this time Nancy was becoming very ill. Fluid was collecting in her lungs, making it very difficult to breathe. Her doctors had warned that she would be in serious trouble if she didn't have dialysis that day, and it was obvious they were right. But we were fighting for something that couldn't wait—a chance for new organs, a once-in-a-lifetime chance that we simply had to take. Now, with the blinding snow raging against us, our hope for that chance was quickly fading. With hours to go before we would reach the hospital, I began to think Nancy would never make it. I felt helpless. The only courage I could muster was in trusting that the Lord would hear our prayers and somehow provide for her.

Suddenly there was a voice on the ham radio—a voice speaking words that could only be heaven-sent. It was the voice of a friend, Rodney Smith, who happened to be in our area, and who just happened to tune in on our desperate attempt to get our daughter to the hospital. I was astounded to hear Rodney asking my husband if we would consider having Nancy flown to Cincinnati! Not only was Rodney a ham operator, he was an accomplished pilot with access to a four-passenger plane. We assured him that we would be thrilled and extremely grateful if he could actually do that. Without a moment's hesitation, he instructed us to meet him at a local airport that we had passed about fifteen miles back.

When we arrived, there was Rodney waiting for us, along with his copilot, Curt Wells. Rodney's boss had graciously allowed him to use his plane, which just happened to be available and ready for takeoff within minutes. Rodney and Curt helped Nancy and me into the plane and my husband went ahead in the car. Things were still very tense as Nancy's condition worsened. She was confused, almost delirious, and was unable to breathe unless I kept pounding her on the back. From the airplane, the copilot called ahead for an ambulance to meet us at the airport and transport us to the hospital. As we were rushed into the ambulance after landing, we gratefully bid farewell to the two kind men who had saved my daughter's life. They wished us well, and said that the flight wouldn't cost us a dime. Helping a friend in need was simply the best way they knew to wish someone a Merry Christmas. And so, miraculously, within one hour of boarding the plane, we were at the University of Cincinnati Medical Center, where preparations were being made for surgery.

Yet our fight was not over. After examining Nancy, the doctors informed us that she would never survive the double-transplant surgery in her present condition. She would first have to be dialyzed—a process that takes four hours. It was after two P.M., and needless to say, this would be cutting it close. Of course, we had no choice but to proceed and pray for the best. She just barely made the seven P.M. deadline for surgery.

My husband finally arrived at the hospital at eight P.M. an hour after the operation had started. I couldn't help but think what the consequences would've been for Nancy if we hadn't had our benevolent airplane rescue.

We sat in the waiting room for hours until, at two A.M. on Christmas Eve morning, the two surgeons emerged, exhausted but gratified. Everything had gone well—our daughter had a new kidney and a new pancreas, which was somewhat of a cure for diabetes. The next morning we were able to see Nancy, who was now breathing normally and looking very healthy. As we held her in our arms, we were convinced of the role God's hand had played over the past twenty-four hours. We would always be indebted to Rodney Smith for tuning us in on his radio that day, but ultimately, we knew there was someone even more powerful who had tuned us in first.

JULIA KELLY
Pikeville, Kentucky

Miles Davis and the Cardboard Man

I DON'T KNOW exactly when he showed up on our street. One day he wasn't there, the next day he was. After a week or two, it seemed like he'd always been there, stumbling around in ratty high-tops, his red beard scraggly, wearing a cardboard sign around his neck that read HUNGRY. HOMELESS. PLEASE HELP. GOD BLESS.

He'd stand at the crowded intersection and stare balefully into drivers' windows. If the light had just turned red and he knew he had some time, he would parade up and down the line of waiting cars, looking hungry and needy.

Every so often a brave soul would barely roll down his window and offer a trembling dollar through the thin slit to the scruffy stranger. The man would take it gratefully, doffing his grease-stained baseball cap and twirling it like a fine country gentleman, in a grand show of gratitude. Meanwhile the cars behind the generous driver would show their disapproval of his naïveté and foolishness by honking an angry refrain.

"Doesn't he know the cardboard man will just use that money for booze and drugs?" the horns seemed to ask.

My wife and I often would complain to each other about the "cardboard man." That's what we called him, for he had no name to us. Indeed, he was barely human in our young, urban professional eyes. He was just another unpleasant pit stop at the intersection on our way home to our eight-hundred-dollar-a-month apartment in a gated community designed to keep out riffraff such as him.

"The cardboard man looked right at me today," my wife would say as she walked through the door carrying her brief-case containing two more hours' worth of marketing research. "He really gives me the creeps. It's like he recognizes me or something."

"He probably does, honey," I would say, looking up from the computer where the rest of my workday was just beginning. "You've always had that effect on older men."

We would laugh. The cardboard man was a daily joke in our house.

We never told each other, however, that the cardboard man's smelly clothes and bushy hair often caused us to roll down our windows and slip him a buck or two despite ourselves, much to the dismay of the honking drivers behind us.

One windy day, succumbing to guilt and rolling down my window, I opened my wallet, only to find that it contained nothing smaller than the eight crisp hundred-dollar bills we planned to use to pay our rent. Months earlier a worker in our supposedly "secure" apartment complex had stolen several residents' checkbooks. Ours had been one of them. We hadn't written a check since.

Thinking fast, I noticed the dented Walkman clipped to the cardboard man's waist and handed him a Miles Davis tape from my cluttered dashboard. His eyes bulged and he snatched it up greedily.

Just then, a gust of wind flew in and out of my window.

It carried away the eight crisp bills I'd set aside for rent.

Traffic zoomed by. I watched helplessly as gusts of exhaust and wind scattered the bills in all directions. The traffic light was still red, cars careened past my front bumper, and the cardboard man and I looked on in horror as each and every bill blew high into the air and slowly disappeared from view.

When the light turned green I pulled into the shopping center next door and ran frantically from corner to corner looking for a sign of my lost rent. I searched everywhere I could reach on foot, but surrounded by strip malls, parking lots, traffic, trees, and shrubbery, I gave up after twenty minutes. It was hopeless. Futile. Silly. My rent was gone. Eight hundred dollars literally thrown to the wind.

My wife was angry when she heard what had happened. But I was even angrier. How could I have been so foolish? Our stomachs lurched as we walked to the fancy clubhouse and explained the situation to our rental agent. She was unsympathetic. There would be late-payment fees. Penalties. Repercussions. Rent was due by the end of the week, period.

Long after my wife had gone to bed, I pored over the meager contents of our checking and savings accounts. Because we had just moved into our apartment and had spent every spare dime on moving expenses and getting our new place set up, we were cash poor. We could not pay our rent. We couldn't even come close.

The next day I watched the road carefully on my way home, hoping for some sign of a stray hundred-dollar bill in the McDonald's parking lot or stuck to the speed-limit sign. But I knew that if I could spot something, someone else would have seen and taken it long before. I didn't see anything green that day. Not even the dying grass in the winter-dry median.

It was only when I got home that I realized I hadn't seen the cardboard man at the intersection. Hmmph, I thought sourly. Probably found one of my hundreds and is off on a bender, listening to Miles Davis and sucking on cheap wine!

The next day was Friday. The end of the week. Rent was due and I slunk by the rental office on my way to work that morning as if they were watching for me. On the way home I was so wrapped up in worry and dread that a knock at my driver's-side window nearly knocked me off of my seat!

There was the cardboard man, smiling at me proudly.

"Oh, I'm sorry," I mumbled. "I don't have anything to give you today."

"I expect not," came a voice that sounded clear and sober. "That's okay, I've got something to give you."

He handed me my Miles Davis tape. My heart sank. Somehow, some way, I had been hoping against hope that . . .

"Go on," he said impatiently. "Open it. You don't think I'd carry around that kind of money and not conceal it, do you?"

Inside the plastic tape case was a wad of hundred-dollar bills. Seven of them, to be exact! "But how—"

"You don't want to know," said the cardboard man, shaking his head proudly. "Took me all day to find them bills. They were stretched out from here to a mile down the road. That's all right," he said, patting his Walkman. "I had Mr. Davis here to keep me company on my travels."

I barely saw the light change through the tears of gratitude in my eyes. I looked at the cardboard man standing straight and tall and as proud as I'd ever seen him. I quickly handed the tape case back to him. He saluted me with a quick wave as I drove off. He was still smiling as I glanced back at him in my rearview mirror. I was amazed that he hadn't tried some angle, let alone just run off with the seven hundred bucks.

Why, he hadn't even asked for a reward!

My very last sight of the cardboard man was of him opening up the tape case and retrieving the crumpled hundred-dollar bill I'd left inside as a thank-you. Neither my wife nor I ever saw him again. You never can tell what clothes your guardian angel will be wearing. For me, it was high-tops and a cardboard sign.

EDWARD ROSMOND
Cocoa Beach, Florida

Santa Was a Jewish Shopkeeper

CHRISTMAS OF 1945 was fast approaching, and it did not promise much cheer for our family. Mom had finally decided to separate from my alcoholic, abusive father. After trying to make the marriage work for so long, now, even with six small children to raise, she knew we would be better off in a home where peace and love would outweigh the prospect of poverty.

It had long been the custom that Mom's three older brothers would come to give her some money to make a little Christmas for us. Very often this support would come at the last minute, but Mom counted on it. This particular year she had gone to a local furniture store that set up a display of toys at the start of the shopping season, and that allowed customers to purchase items on layaway. Carefully planning purchases that would fill the dreams of each of her four girls and two boys, she struggled to put a few dollars down and would pick up the order when her brothers came before Christmas.

My older brother, Edward, and I were probably eleven and twelve years old and had been taken into Mom's confidence to help surprise the little ones. As we waited, day by day, for our uncles to come or for some money to magically appear from any other source, Mom, Edward, and I began to worry that we would not be able to pick up our order.

A few packages that had been given by a charitable organization were hidden in the closet. You know the kind, with anonymous-sounding gift tags that identify the recipient only by sex and age. (I am now sixty-three and still recall that year because I received a package addressed to "girl, age 12." On Christmas morning I opened it to find that it contained two pairs of flannel pajamas for a boy. Many a cold night that winter, I was happy to have those warm flannel pajamas, one pair tan and the other light blue.)

The morning of the twenty-fourth arrived and still we waited. Finally, one by one, Uncle Mick, Uncle Ray, and Uncle John stopped by to wish their kid sister Merry Christmas. They visited for a while, slipped Mom an envelope, and went back to their own secure Christmas homes. Not wanting to reveal how desperately she was depending on their generosity, Mom waited until the last uncle had left and then sent Edward and me to the store where our precious stash awaited.

The problem came when my brother and I walked many, many city blocks only to find that the store had closed early on Christmas Eve. Standing outside the store window, seeing the games and dolls that would have been just what we needed, was more than I could take. It was so cold; it had snowed in recent days. We were obviously not dressed warmly enough for the weather. To console me, Edward suggested that we splurge on trolley fare and get home quicker. The decision to spend fifteen cents on the streetcar was a big deal. This would take us a bit out of our way, but that is what made the difference in the rest of the story.

After taking the number 8 trolley part of the way, we had to change to the number 15 car, which took us along Girard Avenue. In that postwar period, Philadelphia did not have the glamorous look that we see in the malls and Toys "R" Us today. Living in one of the oldest parts of this historic city meant that we were not in the most affluent area. Everywhere you looked you saw darkened, closed stores and very few people out and about.

The lights in a small variety store in the middle of the block were almost not visible. It was Maxie's, a store run by a very elderly Jewish man. It may have been the only store still open in the city that night. My brother and I decided to get off the trolley to see if the store might have any toys. We were thrilled to see he had a small display.

Maxie, his wife and brother-in-law were about to close for the night but agreed to wait while Edward ran the rest of the way home to baby-sit the little ones so that Mom could hurry down to Maxie's. While I waited for her, I went around picking out some things that might fill the needs of our family. When Mom arrived she was so grateful that the shopkeeper had stayed open those extra minutes. We found paper dolls, coloring books with crayons, trucks, and baby dolls. It was not quite what Mom had planned, but she would never have been able to explain why Santa Claus had completely missed our house.

Christmas was not Maxie's holiday to celebrate, but this is just another example of how diversity can be a real blessing. Whenever I retell this story, I marvel at the circumstances that brought the solution. If my brother had not felt sorry for his crying sister and offered to take the trolley home . . . if our route had not taken us past that store . . . and if Santa had not been a Jewish shopkeeper, this Irish Catholic family would not have had a Merry Christmas.

Lovingly composed by one who lived the experience and knows that remembering the difficult times enhances our appreciation of the goodness God gives.

MARIE FOLEY NIELSEN
Toms River, New Jersey

High School Reunion

L WAS EXCITED to be alone with my son, Matthew, for the weekend. We had a good relationship, but I wanted us to have some special time together—a father-and-son vacation. So we went on a "real man's" fishing trip. But while we were gone, what happened at home turned out to be, in the big picture, even more significant.

That weekend my wife, Twilia, and daughter, Heather, decided to make a visit to a nearby church. Having moved recently, we had been searching for a church where our family would feel comfortable worshiping. God had always been part of my life, but because of the church they found that day and the teachings of its pastor, I really began to think about the purpose of life—about faith and love and forgiveness.

I've always known I was a lucky man to have a wife I loved and children I adored. But recently I had been trying to size up my childhood and found myself preoccupied with thoughts of my father—a man I didn't even know, a man who had left me when I was six years old. My parents' divorce had been bitter, and my sisters and I remained with our mother. Dad just suddenly disappeared from our lives, and his absence had left a hole in my young heart. Now, with my own young son to raise, I was thinking more and more about the role of a father, and was seeking to somehow understand what kind of man my father had been.

About this time, in another attempt to better myself, I joined the Masons. I was still feeling the old wounds of my father's abandonment, and although going to church had brought some peace of mind, something was driving me to keep seeking and building on my new relationship with God. Looking back, I believe He was trying to prepare me for what was about to happen.

The day of my discovery unfolded like any other—until I got home from work. I knew something was up by the look in my wife's eye when she met me at the door. "There's a message on the answering machine that I think you'll find very interesting," she remarked as I walked in. Puzzled, I pushed the play button and a voice on the machine said, "Charles Perry, my name is also Charles Perry, and if you'll give me a call, I think you might find that we have something in common."

A thousand thoughts ran through my mind, but one kept coming back: Was this the voice of my father? I had been only six years old when I'd last seen him, and I was now forty-one, so I couldn't tell by his voice. Why would he be calling me, after thirty-five years? Did he want something? Did he have a terminal illness? Was this really my father?

Several years earlier I would've erased the message and never picked up the phone, but because of our new church and my new feelings about love and forgiveness, my heart had softened and I now felt ready. I wondered if this was why I had been thinking recently about whether my father was still alive, and whether he ever thought about me.

Without hesitating, I picked up the phone and dialed the number. A woman answered. I told her my name and asked to speak with Charles Perry. My heart was pounding as I waited. And then I heard an elderly man's voice saying, "I thought it might be you. May I ask you a couple of questions?" I agreed.

"Is your mother's name Shirley?"

"Yes," I answered, my heart beating even faster.

"Do you have two sisters, one named Lola Celeste, and one named Cynthia Leigh?"

Now a lump was forming in my throat. With a shaky voice I answered softly, "Yes."

And then his words: "I am your biological father."

I tried to carry on a normal conversation, like two business acquaintances speaking for the first time. But every few minutes the realization of who I was talking to—for the first time in thirty-five years—hit me and made my knees feel weak. We spoke for about thirty minutes and agreed to meet for lunch the next day. After I hung up, I realized I didn't even know how he had found me. Among a thousand other things I wanted to learn, I made it a point to ask him.

He was inside the restaurant waiting for me when I arrived. As soon as our eyes met, we recognized each other. He stood up and hugged me. It was a little awkward at first, but as the conversation flowed, it began to feel pretty natural. He showed me pictures of my sisters and me at some very early birthday parties, and I could almost remember the feeling of having a dad close to me when I was four and five years old. Questions I had wanted to ask for decades poured out of me. The main one, of course, was, "Why did it take you thirty-five years to find me?"

"Every time I thought about it," he admitted, "I was afraid you'd reject me. It was easier to do nothing. At least that way you couldn't tell me to get lost."

When I finally asked him how he had tracked me down, he told me a story that confirmed my belief in divine intervention and the reality of miracles. It turns out that for many months my father had worked for the local high school as a security aide—the same high school, in fact, that my daughter, Heather, attended. Recently, he had gotten into an interesting discussion with the band teacher, Mr. Tautkus, about becoming a Mason.

At that time Mr. Tautkus knew my father only as "Chuck." He explained to my dad that he had learned about the local lodge through one of his female students whose father had recently joined the Masons. As it turned out, that student was Heather and the father of whom they spoke was me.

As they continued their conversation about this young girl, Mr. Tautkus casually said, "In fact, strange as it may sound, she could pass for your daughter."

"I'm not that young!" remarked my dad. "But how about a granddaughter? What's her name?"

"Heather Perry" was the response.

Looking solemnly into the band teacher's eyes, my father

replied, "My last name is also Perry. Is there any chance you might know her father's name?" Since Mr. Tautkus was well acquainted with my family and me, he said with certainty, "Yes, his name is Charles Perry." And just then the realization hit my dad.

For months, Heather and Chuck, granddaughter and grandfather, had been roaming the same school halls, unaware of their biological link.

When Dad heard this news from the band teacher, he was astounded, strangely excited, and couldn't wait to tell his wife about it as soon as he got home that evening.

"Call him, call him now. Look up his number and let's see what happens," she encouraged. And that was how my family was reunited after thirty-five years of silence and estrangement.

Several months have passed since we were brought together, and it has been a great blessing to us all. Dad lives only three miles away, so we are able to visit often. We've spent our first holidays together, played games together, and are getting to know each other's friends and extended family members. The most meaningful part, though, is that we are now attending church together.

My dad claims that our reunion has brought new life and joy to him and his wife, Helene. For me, it has not only brought resolution to an unfinished piece of my life, it has also added a richness for which I thank God every day.

But mostly, I think it has taught my whole family one of life's most important lessons: It is our great opportunity to forgive and forget those things that have hurt us in the past. For it is only in forgiving that we can lighten our own loads and allow love to rush in where bitterness once was. In the case of my father and me, if God directed our paths to come together after so many years, then certainly, He wants us to love.

CHARLES P. PERRY
Granada Hills, California

Johanna and Emily

ALL PARENTS KNOW how common it is for young children to create imaginary friends to keep them company through the long, idle hours of childhood. Someone to share secrets with, someone to talk to in the backseat of the car—it's all perfectly normal. So we weren't at all alarmed when our daughter Johanna began talking to her imaginary friend, Emily.

Johanna was a little over two and a half when she first began to tell us about her friend Emily. Not wanting to interfere with her creative play, we asked questions about Emily. "What do you do with Emily, sweetie?" my wife, Daisy, and I asked.

"We play, we dance, and we sing," she replied. It sounded like fun to us, and since we were expecting a second baby soon, we chalked up the sudden arrival of Johanna's secret friend to her feelings about the upcoming addition to our family.

Moreover, since we were a military family and had already moved six times in Johanna's short life, we felt it was possible that she had developed an imaginary friend as a way of handling these transitions.

After a while, though, some of her comments about Emily began to puzzle us. "Emily and I were together before," she insisted. "Emily showed me the light." What on earth could she mean by that? More and more often she began to talk about "the light." Where was this place with the beautiful light, where she and Emily had been together before?

As the months passed and Johanna's language skills grew, her stories of Emily became increasingly involved. They also were increasingly told in the past tense—about the things Johanna and Emily had done together before—and the place where they had been together before. In this place that Johanna described, there were lots of other children, too. She couldn't remember their names, though, only Emily's.

"And what did you do when you were with Emily before?" we'd ask.

"Sing and dance." Her stories always involved singing and dancing, and she also told us that all the children in this place could fly.

Johanna's stories remained consistent. For a toddler, she had remarkable recall of the details she'd already revealed about the special place where the children could fly. She gave us vivid descriptions of the light, which seemed to be an important element in this place. Johanna herself seemed to be eerily attuned to light and to the shifting of light throughout the day. Without yet knowing her numbers or the concept of time, she had an uncanny ability to correctly announce what time of day it was. She would be correct within minutes. Even when I would call from a different time zone while traveling, she could always tell me what time it was wherever I was. But what did this all mean?

Daisy and I began to wonder what kind of place Johanna was describing—a place with beautiful light where lots of children sing and dance and fly, waiting to be born. Strange as it seemed, her childlike descriptions of "where she was before" sounded like some sort of prebirth paradise. But once again we shrugged it off, believing that her fantasy world had something to do with her feelings about the new baby coming.

One Saturday afternoon we all piled into the car for a trip to Wal-Mart to do the weekly shopping. Upon entering the store, I began my usual struggle with Johanna, trying to get her to sit quietly in the seat of the shopping cart so that I could buckle the safety strap before we began our shopping. I'd almost gotten the buckle fastened when suddenly Johanna slipped through my hands and stood straight up.

"There she is! Emily is here! That is Emily right over there!" she cried, pointing across the store toward a family pushing two carts full of groceries. The family had four or five children of all ages in tow and were headed toward the parking lot. Daisy and I looked at each other. Should we?

"Do you think it could be her, for real?" she whispered to me as we pushed our cart toward them. "The least we could do is ask." So off we went, walking quickly to catch up with the family before they left the store.

"Excuse me," I asked, "but is one of your children named

Emily?" But I hardly needed an answer. Johanna was already deep in conversation with the youngest of their children, a little girl. Her parents nodded. "Yes, this is Emily here," they replied, pointing to the little girl. But, they asked, why did we want to know? Who were we and how did we know their daughter?

Taking a deep breath, I tried to tell to them about Johanna's stories about "before"—about the place with the light. They looked confused as I spoke, and began to edge away. Sure enough, they *did* think we were crazy, stopping them in the middle of Wal-Mart to tell them our daughters might have known each other before they were born! With a firm hand on her shoulder, Emily's parents began to steer her away from Johanna. But the girls continued to chat happily to each other even as the distance between them grew. It seemed their earthly friendship was not to be. Before the family disappeared out the door, however, Daisy did manage to get Emily's birth date from her mother—September of 1993, just two months before Johanna's.

Johanna continued to talk about her friend, although with less frequency over the next couple of years. But Daisy and I still think about Emily and wonder if there really is a time before birth when special friendships are made. When babies are born, do they still have some vague attachment to the place with the light where children sing and dance and fly—only to have it gradually fade from their memories over the first few years of life?

I guess we'll have to wait to learn the answers to those questions, but in the meantime we are witnessing another special friendship. Our daughter Jessica, born a few months after Johanna met Emily in the store, is two and a half now. When she talks about her close friend Kelly, whom we have never met but whom Jessica claims to have known forever, we don't even question it.

MICHAEL DeSIMONE
Irving, Texas

Rebecca's Touch

HE AIR IN the doctor's office that afternoon was thick and heavy. I was uncomfortably pregnant and very overdue. Beside me, my husband, Cal, struggled quietly with his own pain. The doctor's words cut sharply through the silence: "Mr. and Mrs. Stewart, I am sorry to tell you that Cal has cancer. It is terminal. I hope you live to see the birth of your child."

Was I losing my mind? Did the doctor just say she hoped Cal would live to see the birth of his child? Couldn't she see that I was due to deliver at any moment?

Just three days after that dire diagnosis, on November 19, our daughter was born. Little Rebecca made quite an entrance into our world that night! What a wonderful event it was, in a noisy hospital room full of family, children, and friends. During the whole ordeal, I felt Cal at my side, his arm around my shoulder and his hand on my arm. He was my support, my strength, as he had always been. I had been given a wonderful gift, but little did I know just how precious it would be.

As I held my darling daughter in my arms over the next days and weeks, I celebrated life. As I held my darling husband, I cried about death. The only thing that helped me endure the heartache was this little girl who had been given to us. She was the only light in the darkness of those weeks before Cal's death. Something very real that we could hold on to. Someone who could make us smile. Someone to keep us all going.

It is terrible to watch someone die. The process is unbearable to the person who is suffering, and to the loved ones who struggle with the realization that they won't have this important person in their lives. As the mother of young children, I was deeply concerned about my kids. How would they deal with the loss of their father? Our teenage boys retreated into their rooms to hide their broken hearts. Our six-year-old son would sneak into our bedroom early in the morning to peek at his dad and make sure he was still breathing, still with us. After school he would run up the stairs, two at a time, to his daddy's bedside.

"Daddy? Can I get some fresh water for you?"

"Daddy, are you hungry?"

"Daddy, I love you."

But the day soon came when the bed at home was empty. Cal had been moved to the oncology ward. My husband and I were alone together at the end. I crawled up into the hospital bed with him and tried to express the feelings of my heart. I felt so helpless without him—he had always taken care of me, of all of us. I talked to him for hours, reminding him of the love and laughter we had shared, the dreams, the wonderful experiences of our life together. I thanked him for teaching me by his great example to love, to trust, and to forgive. I thanked him for each of our beautiful children, especially for his last gift—this special part of him that would be in our family when he was gone. She was the precious gift that we could all love, touch, and hold on to.

We were a sight to behold at the funeral—me with a tiny nursing infant, wrapped in a pink flannel blanket, my other children on both sides. I was in a fog, sitting in the church that afternoon. My little son, Tyler, took my hand and said, with tears streaming down his red cheeks, "I wish this was just a dream." Oh, the simple truths in the words of a child. Michael, almost fourteen, sat on my other side. He was hurting and angry, fighting a battle inside that he didn't understand and I didn't know how to help him win. His older brother, Clinton, sat beside him, quiet, suffering, and solemn. And my Rachel, home from college, was an anchor for us all.

Cal's older children conducted the services. Most of them spoke, telling tender stories about their dad. It was touching, but I couldn't feel much, other than the blinding pain of a broken heart. I wondered, How can I possibly be breathing? The pain in my heart should be killing me. Then I felt the baby in my arms as she snuggled in close to me. I held her directly over my ailing heart, feeling the warmth from her small body spread through me like an embrace from Cal. He will always be with me, I realized. Through our children, he will always be with me.

But there were times in the months that followed when I

would have pulled the covers over my head and never come out, had it not been for this soft, warm, sweet little baby who cooed and cuddled at my side, demanding to be fed. What would have become of me—of all of us—if she had not been in our lives? What on earth would the boys have done without her? Michael, always angry, never showed concern for anyone's feelings, as his were so tormented, except when he picked up this little angel. His face would soften, his eyes come alive, when he held her close to his chest. It was the only time he showed any emotion other than anger. He had her to love and to be loved by. Clinton was quiet. He would sneak Rebecca from her bed and take her into his room, holding her tightly. Thinking no one could hear, he cried. He felt safe enough with her to let his emotions out. Tyler played with Rebecca every waking hour, except when one of the other boys was holding her. He read to her, changed her, laughed and sang to her. She filled a void in each of us, an emptiness in our hearts. She was our treasure.

Time rolled on. Days into weeks, weeks into months. After the first year had passed, I finally found myself not holding my breath quite so often. I even began to think about the future, rather than wondering whether I would survive the day! We moved into a new house and made a new beginning. One night, shortly after we had unpacked and organized our belongings, the phone rang. The voice on the line was unfamiliar. "My name is Floris. Someone from your church, named Dennis, asked me to call you. He said you had lost your husband. He had heard that my wife also died of cancer, and he thought perhaps you would like someone to talk with," he explained.

I couldn't believe how easily I shared my thoughts and feelings with this stranger on the phone. That first conversation led to another, and another, and eventually to a "date" for a church function. "Okay," I heard myself saying, "I'll go with you to the meeting at the church on Friday night."

On the day of my date, I began to realize what I had done. What had I been thinking? I had not been on a date since I was nineteen years old, not to mention never having even seen this man! Oh no! What had I done? If only I had taken down his number, I thought, I could call and get out of this mess.

True to his word, he showed up at my door. Well, at least one fear was eliminated as I viewed him through the security door. He didn't look weird. In fact, he was handsome! Then I really got nervous. I hadn't planned on finding another man handsome. I suddenly felt guilty, as if I was doing something wrong. My thoughts were going in many different directions as I sat with my date in the living room, trying to keep Rebecca, who was still nursing, from pulling open my blouse! What a comedy that first night was. I couldn't wait for it to end. The funniest part was when he dropped me off at my door. Clinton was waiting up for us. He hadn't budged from the living room chair until I was home and Floris was gone. He was protecting me!

Floris and I talked almost daily on the phone, and I soon came to feel a close bond with him. The boys were quite reluctant to accept him at first, but Rebecca, only fifteen months old, was delighted by him. Soon it was evident that our feelings for each other were growing stronger and Rebecca again was the one who drew us all together. The boys loved and adored her, as she did them. As they watched her love for Floris grow, they had mixed emotions. Time and time again I watched the love they shared with Rebecca spill over and expand as they saw her bond with Floris deepening. Once again she became a gift, this time a gift for Floris.

Floris and I are now married. And like a lovely ribbon that holds together a beautifully wrapped present, Rebecca has held together our precious family.

CYNTHIA STEWART-COPIER
Roseville, California

Readers might recall Cynthia's moving story "One Last Wish," in the *Christmas Miracles* collection. In it, she related the beautiful and mysterious circumstances of Rebecca's birth. We hope you enjoyed this new story of how the miracle that is Rebecca continued to inspire and unite this special family.

Beyond the Call of Duty

OPERATING A TRAIN through city traffic is never fun. With the crowded conditions, poorly marked intersections, and drivers' errors and misjudgments to contend with, there is always the potential for a wreck. It is even more harrowing when you're behind the controls of a 410,000-pound diesel locomotive. I know. I've been riding in the cab of one for decades now. These engines are beautiful, but just try to stop one quickly. It simply can't be done. There are times when you have to stand on the brakes and pray that it will all turn out okay. One of those times happened just last spring.

My run takes me through the city of Lafayette, Indiana, regularly. On the outskirts of town, the train slows to twenty-five miles an hour and we prepare to make our way across city streets—twenty-four of them. Twenty-four intersections where anything can happen. A meeting between a train and a car on the tracks does not end well, but a meeting between a train and a person is always fatal.

And so, on the afternoon of May 12, 1998, my engineer, Rod Lindley, and I scanned the track ahead of us as we rounded the first curve into town. We spied something lying on the tracks.

"A puppy?" Rod asked, pointing to the mound ahead. He began to toot the horn in an effort to get the animal's attention, despite the fact that sounding the horn was against the railroad's regulations for in-town driving. "Come on, puppy," he muttered under his breath, "move!"

I kept my gaze focused on the object. It could turn out to be just a bundle of rags, I thought to myself. Then I saw it—a tiny little face looking up at the approaching train. "Oh, my God! It's a baby girl!"

Rod reacted quickly, dumping the air on the brakes to make an emergency stop. Never a safe move, it was all the more risky that day because of our cargo—liquid propane gas. With explosive gas on board, a derailment in the middle of an urban area would be a large-scale disaster. He pressed his hand to the horn, which sounded one continuous wail as we felt the train shudder underneath us. The engine jolted forward and we felt the railcars behind us smash into each other as the train began to slow. It was slowing down, but not fast enough to stop before we would be upon the little girl. It seemed certain that we would kill her.

Without thinking, I yanked open the door to the cab and stepped out onto the narrow walkway that skirts the engine. I have never been involved in a fatal accident in all the years I have worked for the railroad. And I wasn't going to start now. I hung tightly on to the safety rail as the train continued to buck and jolt beneath my feet. I didn't have much of a plan in mind except somehow to save the girl and not be thrown off the train in the process. As I reached the front of the cab and stood at the edge looking down onto the swiftly moving track beneath me, I saw my only chance—the snowplow. As every schoolchild knows, the wedge-shaped snowplow on an engine is designed to throw obstacles out of a train's path. And that's what it would do if it reached the baby before I did. Whenever there is an incident between a train and something else, the train always wins.

We continued to gain on the baby. I saw her roll slightly off the tracks, but not far enough off to avoid being hit altogether. The only way she would not be hit would be if she continued to lie down. But suddenly I saw her raise her backside, preparing to stand. "No, no, baby, lie down!" I yelled. The train had slowed to fifteen miles an hour, but we still couldn't stop it.

Suddenly, like a light switching on in my brain, a clear plan formed in my mind. I climbed down as close to the edge of the snowplow as I could. By standing on one leg on my toes, holding on with just one hand and stretching my other leg out as far as possible, I might be able to kick her out of the way as we passed by. But I would only have a split-second chance . . .

We were upon her. I took my one shot, sweeping her aside with my foot as the train passed. I saw her fall and hit some rocks before her body spun around back toward the train. Had she fallen far enough away, or had we hit her? I jumped from the slowing train and ran back to her. She lay crying by the tracks, her head bleeding. But the blood was from a sharp rock, not from the train. Incredibly, we hadn't hit her at all!

"Mama, Mama!" she cried as I lifted her from the dirt. "Okay, sweetheart," I whispered as I brushed the dirt from her face, "let's go find Mama."

As I walked from the tracks with this beautiful crying baby in my arms, I saw a policeman running toward me from the road. I could tell he was visibly relieved to hear her screams. Not long after, the paramedics arrived. They tried to take her from my arms, but she held on to my bib overalls and cried even louder. So I went with them to take the baby to the local hospital for some stitches and to be reunited with her mother. I later found out that the baby, nineteen-month-old Emily, had gotten out of the house, escaped from her back garden, and traversed some fifty yards to the unfenced train tracks, unbeknownst to her mother, who was gardening in the front yard.

I don't know why little Emily escaped near-certain death with only a chipped tooth and some stitches, but every time I think back to that little baby and what might have happened, I know I was part of a miracle. Something must have been guiding us though Lafayette last year—orchestrating our every move—and I think it was more than just the train's tracks.

ROBERT MOHR
Denver, Indiana

The Search for Israel

EFORE TOM, THERE was Israel. What I mean is, before I met and married my husband, Tom, my significant other was Israel. Who was a cat. A black Siamese cat. Now, I know that there are many single women out there who are smiling and nodding in recognition: "Yes, that's right, my boyfriend is a cat, too." Where would we be without the love, warmth, entertainment, and companionship of our kitties on some of those lonely nights at home? With no children or husband in my house, it was Israel that I nurtured.

When I married Tom, Israel came along, too, even if it meant trading in the familiar comforts of my longtime home for the new and (to me and Israel) exotic experience of life in a small mountain community.

Not long after the wedding gifts were opened and my bridal gown was dry-cleaned, Tom accepted a job building a house in the tiny town of Trinity Center, California. This beautiful town of just a few hundred folks is nestled at the base of the majestic Trinity Alps, a mountain range that many compare to the Swiss Alps. The area draws tourists from around the world to hike and to fish the crystal-clear water of Trinity Lake. I looked forward to living in a more rural setting than the one I'd grown up in. To breathe the crisp night air and gaze at a starlit sky instead of weaving through car-clogged roads and watching the sun set in a haze of smog . . . ah, heavenly.

But with rural mountain charms came rural mountain dangers, and it wasn't long before I realized that Israel would have to be an indoor cat from now on. How would a city-bred kitty ever stand up against mountain lions, coyotes, skunks, and whatever else lay in wait outside in the darkness? No, Israel would just have to learn to pass the time lounging indoors near the woodstove.

Our lives quickly settled into a routine. Every morning I would rush happily around our little house, making breakfasts and packing lunches for me, Tom, and my nine-year-old stepson Jayson. Jayson loved his new mountain school, and I loved being able to help Tom build the new house out at the job site—hammering, sawing, and hauling lumber until we returned home happy but exhausted at the end of the day. My morning routine was always dampened, though, by the endless attempts that Israel would make to try to sneak out any door or window that was left open. A born prankster who had kept me amused with his endless tricks during my single days, he soon transferred all of his energy and skill to trying to break out of this tiny mountain cabin and run for the beckoning hills. One day he finally succeeded.

On my way out the door on that particular morning, I noticed that Israel was not at his usual post waiting to try to squeeze outside past my leg. Was he back in his spot by the woodstove? I checked, but there was no sign of him. I checked the other rooms. Nothing. My heart racing, I rushed outside to search the yard. No black kitty anywhere. Just big green mountains and trees as far as the eye could see.

For three long days I searched for Israel. From neighbor to neighbor I walked, teary-eyed, to ask if anyone had seen him. "How long has he been gone, didya say?" they'd ask. And then they'd shake their heads in sorrow. "If one of the big cats didn't get him, the cold surely will." Israel's fate—to be eaten by a mountain lion or frozen to death—was no mystery to the folks who'd lived in the mountains for years.

But Israel's fate—Israel's safety—meant everything to me. After all of those years together, I couldn't just shrug and give him up to the wild. So I prayed. I prayed for Israel's safe return the same way that mothers say prayers when their sons go off to battle, the way that we pray when seeing our loved ones off at the airport. I prayed to God that my little kitty would come home again. And on the third day that Israel was missing, I heard an answer. A voice in my heart told me that Israel would return on the seventh day, just before midnight.

I have a simple faith. I believe in God and trust that He cares for me more than I may ever know, and that His love extends to all of the earth's creatures. I trusted that the voice I had heard spoke the truth. I was simply to believe, and to wait.

Exactly seven days from the day Israel disappeared, after Tom and Jayson had both gone to bed, I settled into a rocker near the woodstove and fixed my eyes on the spot where Israel usually slept. Some time before midnight tonight, I thought happily to myself, Israel will come home.

The clock ticked loudly; the chair squeaked on the wooden floor as I nervously rocked back and forth. A log crackled in the stove. The hours dragged by. Worn out from a long day of construction work, I struggled to keep my eyes open. I checked the clock for the hundredth time; it was eleven-thirty. And then I nodded off.

I awoke to a faint sound, the sound of a kitty crying. "Israel!" I threw open a window and shouted his name again. "Israel, is that you?" A weak meow was my answer. Racing to the front door, I threw it open. There on the front porch was Israel. Bedraggled, matted, dirty, and bloodied, holding one injured paw ahead of him as he walked, Israel had come home. My simple faith and trust were rewarded, and I knew that God's love truly does extend to all of the earth's creatures. The little black cat whose name I had chosen from the Bible returned seven days after he left, at a quarter to twelve.

CAROL RITENOUR
Granite Bay, California

God's Perfect Gift

L AWOKE THAT morning to the usual sound of steady drizzle on the roof overhead. As is typical for Washington in December, we had seen days of gray skies and cold rain. After dressing, I hurried out to the living room to stoke the woodstove so as to warm the house before the children awoke.

Rounding the corner into the living room, I stopped to admire the fourteen-foot silver fir draped with five strands of twinkling miniature lights. For a brief instant I felt my heart leap into pre-Christmas excitement, only to be immediately replaced by the dull ache which had become so familiar.

After stoking the fire, I crossed the living room to check on five-month-old baby Jessica, who was asleep in her crib. As I gazed at her angelic face, I couldn't help but marvel at how beautiful she was. Perhaps the combination of brown eyes and the reddish tint to her hair made her especially striking.

Seeing that she was sleeping soundly, I grabbed a stack of unopened Christmas cards and sat down on the couch, determined to read them.

About halfway through the stack, I came upon a card from a friend whom I hadn't heard from in years. Included in her card was a letter recounting the highlights of the past year. It had been a good year for them: a job promotion for her husband, a move to a new house, her career finally taking off, and their children doing well. Her letter was very much like the other cards that I had read, but the words at the end of her letter stopped me cold. She had signed her letter: "Isn't our God good!"

For a moment my heart was too frozen for me even to comprehend her closing words. If the goodness of God was evident in all the gifts he had given them, what kind of God did I have?

Our year had been anything but good. It had begun with the devastating loss of our savings account, followed by the closing of the door to Joel's dream job, and spending the last three months of my pregnancy extremely ill. Even though these things had been hard, they were nothing compared with the darkness of the tunnel that we found ourselves in now.

Two months earlier we had learned that our precious baby girl Jessica was dying of a terminal brain disorder, cause and cure unknown. For five years we had longed and prayed for this baby, only to find that she had but months to live. Our hearts were in unspeakable agony as we faced the valley of the shadow of death, which lay somewhere ahead of us.

Still brooding over the closing words of the letter, I put the stack of Christmas cards down and headed into the kitchen to fix breakfast.

As I entered the kitchen, my gaze fell on the old microwave sitting on the counter. Our microwave had given out a few days earlier and the previous night a gracious friend had brought us her old one. Seeing that it needed cleaning before it could be used, I began to scrub it out.

As I worked, my mind drifted back over the events of this past year. Even though we had experienced loss, disappointment, sickness, and now tremendous sorrow, had we not also seen the goodness of God in our lives? If Joel had taken a new job as he had hoped to, we would have been in far worse trouble. The new job was located in a remote town and lacked good health-insurance benefits. At the time it had been a terrible disappointment, but now, with a terminally ill child with tremendous medical needs, it was evident that God had been protecting us. Even now, as my mind retraced the events of the past two months, I could remember numerous times when we had seen God's tender loving care surrounding us. Yes, we had experienced His goodness in the most unexpected ways, but what about our little Jessica? How would I ever be able to see the goodness of God in the way that He had created her?

Just then the groggy voice of my six-year-old daughter broke into my thoughts: "Mommy, what's for breakfast?" Looking up from my cleaning project, I saw Ginny climb down the loft ladder from her bedroom above the kitchen. Her waist-length blond hair was in a braid that was fuzzy from being slept on. She wore pink Barbie pajamas, and her blue eyes still had a sleepy look.

As soon as Ginny entered the kitchen, she spotted the old microwave. Her eyes flew wide open. She let out an excited squeal, and a huge grin spread across her face. "Oh, Mommy," she said. "A new microwave!" I tried to explain to her that it was really just an old microwave from a friend's garage, but her excitement was not dampened and she continued to comment on its pretty color and other fine features.

Suddenly Ginny stopped her excited chatter about the microwave and turned to me and said, "Oh, Mommy, I think we are God's most favorite family."

Curious as to what she was thinking, I asked her, "What makes you say that?"

"Mommy, when we wanted a pony, God gave us a pony!" Ginny began. "When we needed a pretty Christmas tree, God helped us get up the mountain safely to find the tree! Now when we needed a microwave, God gave us a microwave! And Mommy, best of all, when we prayed for a baby, God gave us a baby—even though she is a little broken!"

No sooner had Ginny completed her statement than she turned on her heel and headed into the living room to examine the gifts under the Christmas tree. With Ginny's words still ringing in my ears, I just stood there, unable to move.

I pondered each of the gifts that Ginny had thought showed God's special love for us. The pony was twenty-four years old and had problem feet. Our Christmas tree was beautiful, but we had weathered a mountain to cut it ourselves.

The microwave worked, but it was very old, and yes, God had given us our precious baby, but as Ginny had put it, she was broken. How was it that Ginny had seen the goodness of God in each of these gifts, but all I had seen were their outward imperfections?

Suddenly it struck me! Ginny's words had been, "*God* gave us a pony! *God* gave us a tree! *God* gave us a microwave! *God* gave us a baby!" What Ginny had been doing was focusing on the fact that each gift had been given to us by God. By focusing on Him, she was able to see them as good and perfect gifts. My focus was on the darkness and pain all around me, which made it impossible to see the goodness of God in any of the gifts that He had given us.

Still pondering Ginny's words, I headed back into the living room to check on Jessica. Stopping in the doorway, I took in the beautiful Christmas scene in the living room: the warm fire crackling in the corner, Ginny crouched down rattling each gift under the sparkling silver fir, and Jessica sound asleep in her crib.

Crossing the room to Jessica's crib, I quietly stood next to my sleeping baby. I studied her beautiful features and silently thanked God that this Christmas I still had her to love and hold. If only I could do what Ginny had done, which was to keep my eyes fixed on God. Then, even in the Christmases to come, when my sweet baby's face would be but a memory etched in my heart, I'd be able to look back and see that although Jessica's little body may have been broken, her spirit was a lesson in love to all of us. As Ginny had taught me, her life was truly God's perfect gift.

God's Perfect Gift

Every good and perfect gift is from above,
Coming down from the Father of the heavenly lights,
Who does not change like shifting shadows.

—James 1:17

In loving memory of our baby Jessica Marie.

MARY LEISY
Redmond, Washington

Do you have a miracle you would like to share? We are putting together more books about miracles. We would love to hear about the miracle in your life. Please send your story to:

Jennifer Basye Sander
Big City Books
"Miracles"
P.O. Box 2463
Granite Bay, CA
95746-2463

Please include your address and phone number so we can contact you.

$\mathcal{A}CKNOWLEDGMENTS$

O MANY PEOPLE have helped us with the "miracle books" over the past three years, and we are deeply grateful for all they have done for us. Once again, we thank our agent Sheree Bykofsky, our editor Toni Sciarra, and our other friends at William Morrow & Company. You are all irreplaceable.

Hundreds of people have shared their stories with us over the years. We'd like to thank the following for helping make this book a reality:

Edward Andrusko, the Arfsten family, Frank Baranowski, the Basye family, Carole Bellacera, Randall Cone, Chris Conkling, Cynthia Stewart-Copier, Sherry Crum, Michael and Daisy DeSimone, Bob Dreizler, Rusty Fischer, Terry Foley, Hope Gardner, Bobby Gawthrop, the Glassover family, Diane Goldberg, Mark Victor Hansen, Hilary Hinkley, Starr Hughes, Michelle Hurst, Azriela Jaffe, Marlene Jannusch, Connie Jones, Maureen Keeney, Julia Kelly, Marlene King, Helen Kinzeler, Polly Kreitz, Laura Lagana, Mary Leisy, the Lewis family, Lucy Whitsett McGuire, Debbie McLellan, Roberta L. Messner, the Miller family, Robert and Cathy Mohr, Marie Foley Nielsen, Charles P. Perry, Barbara and John Pitcavage, Carmen Leal-Pock, George E. Raley, Jr., Christina Richter, Guy Sagi, Gil Sanchez, Mette Hansen Schaer, Margaret H. Scanlon, Michael Stein, Mike Tidwell, Laura Walker, James and Reda Wallace, and Mary Ann Ziakas.